Tempus CHANGING TIMES *Series*

Bristol Times
revisited

Tempus CHANGING TIMES *Series*

Bristol Times
revisited

David Harrison

TEMPUS

Play the game: A picture of a village cricket team in or near Bristol, which was found in the papers of a former Bedminster woman. A lovely range of head gear – but where is it?

Frontispiece: Arcady. Bristol had two attractive shopping arcades, the Upper and Lower, before the last war. The Upper was blitzed but the Lower is still there today.

First published 2003

Tempus Publishing Limited
The Mill, Brimscombe Port,
Stroud, Gloucestershire, GL5 2QG

British Library Cataloguing in Publication Data.
A catalogue record for this book is available from the British Library.

ISBN 0 7524 2844 6

Typesetting and origination by Tempus Publishing Limited
Printed in Great Britain by Midway Colour Print, Wiltshire

Contents

Big guns. One of the two cannons which used to dominate the bottom of the Cabot Tower, on Brandon Hill, before they were scrapped to help the war effort in 1943. They had been on show there since the Crimean war in 1857.

Acknowledgements

My thanks go to: Gerry Brooke, indefatigable *Evening Post* researcher, who has tracked down most of the photographs and helped set up the scanning for this and the last *Bristol Remembered* book; Michelle Smith, who worked in her own hours to scan the images for this and the last 'Bristol Times' collection. Mike Lowe, editor of the *Evening Post*, and Rob Stokes, assistant editor, for use of company equipment and time; Matilda Pearce, our local history team contact at Tempus Publishing, for enthusiastic and friendly support; our loyal and supportive readers and contributors, a constant source of surprise and inspiration, and lastly the local historians, writers and archivists, especially the few whose work is a beacon to all of us.

Introduction

Welcome to another collection of some of the best and most interesting items from the five years that 'Bristol Times' has been an essential part of the *Evening Post*.

As I said in volume one, the 'Bristol Times' started as a way of offering something for our many older readers. It was quite a shock when it was welcomed wholeheartedly by readers of all ages and it has become one of the best read parts of the paper. In fact it has been so successful that this year we decided to increase publication to twice a week. The familiar Tuesday edition – a friend to so many – will be staying as it is but there is now a Saturday 'Bristol Times Two' which focuses on the years from the 1960s to today – years we have, admittedly, neglected a little in the original supplement. So perhaps at a later date there might even be a 'Best of Bristol Times Two' although it's probably some years off with so much to be saved in book form from its older sister.

This anthology concentrates largely on articles from 1998, the first year of 'Bristol Times'. The five-year gap means some of them have had to be tweaked to get rid of their links to a particular time or event but, that apart, they are as originally printed. If you have a particular favourite you would like to see in any future volume, do write and let us know.

Bristol is changing all the time, of course, and residents of a city left ruined after the war would scarcely recognise what has been done to the old place. Some of the changes, like the harbour development and @Bristol, are positive and add immeasurably to the atmosphere of the city. To stroll around the quaysides on a warm summer day, enjoying the crowds and the activities and the attractions is a wonderful experience which few other comparable cities can match.

Some are not so good – the terrible, soulless office blocks built in the 1960s, the much-disliked centre which looks like a leftover from the Communist era in some eastern European city, the late-night noise and violence that seems to come built in to every new bar and pub. Before the Second World War, King Street was not a place where decent folks went on a Saturday night. These days, walking to the tiny handful of establishments that welcome all age groups has the same menacing feeling of trekking through the jungle. However, that isn't really Bristol's fault, although perhaps the council could have tipped the balance slightly away from the endless drinking holes to a mix of attractions for all age groups and not just students. As it stands this is 'Youth City' and the centre is no place for anyone over 21 on a Saturday night. That is sad. Excepting all this, the Bristol of 2003 is immeasurably better than the one we inherited after the Second World War. Imagine there being nowhere to eat but the odd British Restaurant, little on the menu but meat and two veg, and nowhere for the young to spend evenings but hearty Christian youth clubs or semi-military groups like the Boys Brigade, which offered table tennis and advice on growing up ('Be clean in thought, word and deed' as the old Scout oath used to say). Clothes were drab and dull and children dressed like small replicas of their parents or wore awful wide-legged shorts and ties on every occasion. There was no television, but that didn't really matter because the radio (all BBC and Radio Luxembourg then, of course) offered such top-class fare.

There was Jet Morgan and his sterling crew of typecast astronauts battling flying saucers; the eerie *Voice Of Hesikos*, the anarchic humour of *The Goons*. Old stars of the music hall and screen found a new career for their autumn years on the wireless (Gert and Daisy, Sandy Powell, Rob Wilton, Bebe Daniels) while the newer generation of comedians appealed more to younger tastes.

Bristol Old Vic had dream cast lists of names, who would go on to become the biggest stage stars of their generation while the Hippodrome attracted crowds of thousands for personal appearances by legends such as Margaret and Julia Lockwood. Only those who were there tend to remember them today.

And that's really what *Bristol Times Revisited* is all about – reminding older readers of what life was about as Britain struggled back to normal after the war and informing younger ones of the brighter moments, the highlights of a fairly bleak era. How many who weren't even born then can imagine the stultifying boredom of music, pre-rock 'n' roll where jolly groups like the Stargazers and melodramatic balladeers such as Johnny Ray, Frankie Laine, David Whitfield and Jimmy Young vied for chart honours with novelty entertainers like Guy Mitchell and Lita Roza and big band veterans like Anne Shelton and Frank Sinatra? How many these days realise it was the youngsters in the 1960s who invented the teenager, breaking free of the stultifying mini-adult dress code and abandoning their parents' music, together with their parents clothes and morals. It was a good time to be alive and 'Bristol Times' wants to reflect that, as well as the very different life for the average Briton in the 1920s and '30s.

The supplement is meant as a celebration of the way life was lived in the past without it being distorted by rose-coloured glasses.

The generation that lived before the war is getting older and smaller these days and unless their memories of what life was like for them are recorded now, much valuable first-hand social history will be lost. We try to do our bit in preserving that evidence, leavened with a dose of entertaining tales from history. What you have in your hand is a small sample of our output so you can judge for yourself.

David Harrison

1 Quirks and Oddities of History

Quirks and oddities

Tank Warfare in the First World War – as it didn't happen!

The following is a romanticised account of a dramatic tank attack during the First World War when the primitive diamond-shaped mobile guns gave the British a huge advantage in the muddy fields of France. The whole report is fictional. It comes from the *BEF Times* (British Expeditionary Force) which combined serious, if censored, reporting

with satire on the war and the officers in charge. One delightful spoof advertisement offered 'the very latest thing in trench coats with a flounced moire lining and dainty motifs,' and added a fashion alert: 'Send at once, or you'll be late. A soldier must be up to date'. The report is preserved on a faded clipping found in a First World War diary by a descendant of a Bristol Tommy who has asked to remain anonymous. It was credited to Teech Bomas and is a parody of the flamboyant style and colourful exaggerations of the *Daily Mail*'s Man at the Front, William

Ready for action. An Allied tank at the Battle of Amiens in 1918. The beam lying across the top was linked to the tank track and could be moved around to give the vehicle some solid footing in the atrociously muddy conditions.

Beach Thomas. Whoever 'Our Special Correspondent' was, he seemed to enjoy spectacular words, too – this is probably the first time 'progolodymythorus' and 'proglodomyte' appeared in the *Evening Post*! Any offers on what they mean?

'The Tanks Went Over', by Our Special Correspondent:

In the grey and purple light of a September morn, they went over. Like great prehistoric monsters they leapt and skipped with joy when the signal came. It was my great good fortune to be a passenger on one of them. How can I clearly relate what happened? All is one chaotic mingling of joy and noise. No fear! How could one fear anything in the belly of a perambulating, peripatetic progolodymythorus? Wonderful, epic, on we went, whilst twice a minute the 17-inch gun on the roof barked out its message of defiance.

At last we were fairly among the Huns. They were round us in millions and in millions they died. Every wag of our creature's tail threw a bomb with deadly precision, and the mad, muddled, murderers melted. How to describe the joy with which our men joined the procession until at last we had a train 10 miles long. Our creature then became in festive mood and, jumping two villages, came to rest in a crump-hole. After surveying the surrounding country, from there we started rounding up the prisoners. Then with a wag of our tail (which accounted for 20 Huns), and some flaps with our fins, on we went. With a triumphant snort, we went through Bapaume, pushing over the church in a playful moment, and then steering a course for home, feeling that our perspiring, panting proglodomyte had thoroughly enjoyed its run over the disgruntled, discomfited, disembowelled earth. And so to rest in its lair, ready for the morrow and what that morrow might hold. I must get back to the battle.

Mad Carew and the Green Eye of the Little Yellow God

Do you remember these catchy lines?
'He was known as Mad Carew by the subs of Kathmandu.
He was hotter than they felt inclined to tell;
But for all his foolish pranks, he was worshipped in the ranks,
And the colonel's daughter smiled on him as well.'

Back in the days before radio, television and dining out, there were music halls and simple home-made entertainment. A great delight of both was the dramatic recitation of a blood-stained ballad, a sentimental tale of dying children, or something of an improving nature. Of all the monologues and parlour poems, the favourite of all which is still much loved today was *The Green Eye of the Little Yellow God*. A local couple, Jenny and John Haskins from Kingsdown, have visited the place where this lurid tale of love and revenge was set – and discovered it may well have been based on fact. 'I was quite amazed,' says Jenny. 'I had always thought it was a melodramatic round-the-piano piece which someone had just made up after reading Rudyard Kipling. But it does seem that the writers must have talked to someone who was out in Kathmandu and that the poem may have some basis in fact.'

The Green Eye of the Little Yellow God was written by Milton Hayes and Cuthbert Clarke around 1911 and has the famous opening line, 'There's a one-eyed yellow idol to the north of Kathmandu'. The story tells of Mad Carew, a madcap junior officer much given to pranks who loved the colonel's daughter 'with the passion of the strong'. On her 21st birthday, he asks her what she wants as a gift from Mad Carew. The capricious wench replies that nothing but the green eye of the little yellow god will do. That night, while the birthday dance is in full swing, Mad Carew staggers back to barracks with his shirt and tunic torn and a bloody gash across his

An ancient ceremony. A Nepalese king is enthroned in the old Kathmandu palace. Was this where the Little Yellow God flourished?

head. He presents the green eye to the colonel's daughter who, rather wisely as it turns out, refuses to accept it. Mad Carew is left to sleep off his larcenous adventure and is found next morning with a knife buried in his heart. 'T'was the vengeance of the little yellow god'. The poem ends with the broken-hearted colonel's daughter tending his grave above the town and no doubt wishing she'd asked for something simpler like an elephant or a gold navel plug.

It is a great melodrama which demands to be read aloud, as Bransby Williams did on a very early gramophone record with ringing, doom-filled tones. When the *Evening Post* did a survey a few years ago of favourite parlour poetry and music hall monologues, the Little Yellow God won hands (or green eyes) down.

Now Kathmandu is in Nepal, and Nepal was never part of the British Empire. But it did have an official British Resident and a few soldiers to ward off the less than welcoming Nepalese. Could Mad Carew have been one of them? Jenny and John

discovered on a visit there that there is, as the poem states, a graveyard of little marble crosses below the town. More intriguingly, there is a shrine to a goddess called Vajira Yogini to the north of Kathmandu, and she is gilded a yellow colour and is said to possess a third eye made from emerald. The Colonel's daughter could have been the daughter of the British Resident or of a senior soldier just passing through, while the Residency (now the Indian Embassy) was certainly big enough for a grand ball.

The music would have been provided by a piano or a huge gramophone, brought on the backs of porters through the high passes between India and Nepal. Mad Carew was probably discovered because of the sophisticated burglar alarm of bells with which the shrine was rigged, even in his day. 'It does all seem to add up,' says Jenny. 'Certainly the atmosphere of the place reflects the mood of the poem and you can imagine exactly where everything is supposed to have happened.

We did ask, but no one in Kathmandu could recall a British officer being murdered at this time, which would have been a major event in the days of the Raj. Perhaps the regiment that was serving there at the time might have a record.'

There is only one drawback – Hayes and Clarke never went to Kathmandu and probably not even as far as India. That leaves two possibilities; firstly that they picked up a true story from a soldier or civilian who was there, or secondly that the whole thing is an uncanny coincidence. God and Her green eye, eh!

Kipes and putchers along the Severn

Kipes, putts, putchers and vor'eels – how many people today would even know which trade they were used in, let alone what they were?

At one time, they were common along the Severn and can still be seen in some places at this time of the year. Kipes (sometimes called putts) were what the salmon fishermen called fixed engines – huge wickerwork baskets lined up across the river to take anything that moved, from shrimps to giant sturgeon. The kipe was, strictly speaking, the six-foot wide mouth of the engine. The waist was the butt, while the narrow (and detachable) end was the forewell or vor'eel. The vor'eel was blocked with kelp (seaweed) to stop the fish escaping.

There were smaller, openwork baskets, used solely for salmon, called putchers, while the curved baskets in which fishermen took home their catch was a welch or a witcher. Basket fishing involved placing the fixed engines in a V-shape with a basketwork fence called a leader or hedge to guide salmon into the mouth of the kipes. Lewis Wilshire, who waded out into the middle of

Fishy Business. Fisherman Fred Bennett checks his putchers for River Severn salmon in this picture of 50 years ago. Fish have been caught this way since Saxon times.

the Severn in 1953 to take some now-historic photographs, wrote in his book *Berkeley Vale and Severn Shore:*

'The kipe is the most efficient method ever devised for fishing with fixed engines. It will catch anything from a shrimp to a sturgeon, yet its history goes back thousands of years.

'Lave net fisherman Bob Knapp of Oldbury told me he had found old kipes of great antiquity when the river current scoured out part of a bank in which they were buried.'

Lave nets were another Severn speciality. These were huge nets described by writer Brian Waters as 'a noble weapon of great antiquity, the last true hunting weapon used in Britain today'. Fishermen spotted the salmon from boats and pursued them on foot

Salmon supper. Woven from hazel and withy, these special baskets are able to withstand the strong ebb and flow of the waters of the river. These two salmon were caught at Aust, near the old ferry crossing.

Wickerwork. John Walters, who fished the Severn Estuary for more than 25 years, checks his putchers for the coming season.

Muddy waters. Old fishing stakes line the river bank near the first Severn Bridge.

Flixed engines. Kipes, as the baskets are also known, are exposed at low tide at Salmon Lodge, in this 1958 picture. This part of the river, near Oldbury-on-Severn, is now part of the reservoir for Oldbury nuclear power station.

Ancient heritage. Old salmon baskets piled high at Littleton-on-Severn. People have used this method of fishing for generations, but how much longer can this ancient tradition continue?

along sandbanks. The nets were held under water until the lave-netter sensed a fish was in it. Then it was scooped out, killed with a blow from a rock staff or knocker, and stored in a rock pool while the next was hunted. There was a place called Salmon Pool not far from Oldbury where, many centuries ago, fishermen built The Standings – great blocks of stone on which the lave netter stood to watch for fish. Amazingly, much of this fishing went on at night and there was no room for error. As the tide races in, the water level can rise nearly six feet in as many minutes, and many fishermen were drowned when they left it too late to leave. Further up the Severn, around Framilode, the catch was

In the bag. Salmon fisherman Dave Bennett opens his sack and deposits yet another prize catch.

elvers – young eels which run the river in their millions and were traditionally caught with three foot by two foot elver nets on a five foot pole.

Pollution and over fishing have changed the face of Severn fishing as much as anything. Lewis Wilshire records that at the turn of the century, the average salmon catch from nets was 24,140 fish. By 1940, it was down to 4,294, and it dropped even further before a slight upturn as the river became cleaner.

The days when postmen carried guns

Charles Theodore Baker was a man who made his mark when the Wild West meant the West of England, and postmen to Cheddar went armed.

At just 21 Charles Theodore Baker set up his own business in Weston-super-Mare, borrowing £25 from a trusting elder brother to buy a pony chair which he hired out to visitors.

That was in 1889, when Weston, once a little fishing village, had been transformed by the railways into the Queen of the Somerset coast. It was the ideal place for a tourist business in those less-demanding days, and Charles Theodore prospered. He bought additional horses and cabs and stabled them behind No. 38 Locking Road in what today is a modern workshop. Baker hired out coachmen, horses and broughams (one-horse closed carriages) to the residents of Weston and to doctors who used his horses and cabs for house calls. He still had an eye for a main chance – he won a Royal Mail contract to deliver the post twice daily to the Cheddar valley. It seems incredible but just 90 years ago the area was so wild that his coachmen had to carry pistols to guard against the robbers that infested the area. One of the original pistols and a photograph of the intrepid coachman is on show in the Weston office of Bakers Dolphin, the travel company that grew from the tiny pony hire business.

Charles Theodore expanded into the funeral business as well, providing single or double-horse broughams and carriages to local undertakers. They offered a first, second or third class funeral to reflect the social status of the deceased. He carried on expanding until the First World War when all his horses were commandeered by the army. By 1918, the day of the horse was nearly over, and doctors and undertakers had their own cars. Thus, Charles Theodore turned to motorized transport too, even on the dangerous Cheddar mail service, as well as offering hearses and funeral limousines. In 1923, Baker bought his first charabanc and painted it bright red to match his Royal Mail fleet. Travelling in them must have been daunting – they had solid rubber tyres and only a removable canvas cover to protect against the rain. Passengers had to get on and off by clambering up and down steps placed against the side of the coach. Still, they carried up to 20 passengers at a storming 25mph – more than enough for the narrow roads of the time. Charles' next venture wasn't quite so successful. He opened a seafront booking office and offered a programme of sightseeing tours for holiday-makers. Unfortunately he chose to do it in 1939, just before war broke out.

The coaches were contracted to British Empire Airways (later BOAC) to carry air crews around Britain. In 1945 Charles' sightseeing tours finally took off, and the Weston Greys fleet of coaches was launched. Bakers took over Atyeo's Pride of the West fleet and later the Weston branch of the big Bristol operator, Wessex. By then, Charles Theodore had died, aged eighty-two, but his company continued, merging with Dolphin Travel in 1984 and becoming one of the major players in the industry. Not bad for an initial £25 investment!

Jeffrey Archer, Time Lord

Still mounted on the wall above the Corn Exchange in Corn Street is unique evidence of what happens when man tries to mess about with time.

It is a clock with three hands – one for the hour and two for the minutes, and it goes back to a time of chronological anarchy which Lord Archer's plan could revive in a small way. Lord Archer of Weston-super-Mare was campaigning to get England and Scotland placed in different time zones before his little problem with the Law. It shows he didn't know his history and the chaos created by every provincial town keeping its own time, usually worked out by a local resident with some scientific knowledge.

Even when stagecoaches were introduced, it made little difference that Bristol and London were 10 minutes or so apart. But when the railways and the electric telegraph arrived, disaster loomed. All the new railways which ran to or from London decided to adopt Greenwich Mean Time (GMT) right across their systems. So, as Bristol and London time was 10 minutes different, the problems were obvious.

Passengers found themselves arriving in Bristol on (GMT) time, but too late for connections which had also left on time – Bristol time. Numerous complaints got nowhere and even in London itself there was a difference of two minutes between the east and west ends of the city. But the problem got worse the further you got from London.

BRISTOL – The Corn Exchange

Timeless sight. The clock on Bristol's Corn Exchange, which works by a series of weights and pulleys, actually has TWO minute hands.

Just a minute. A little extra time at the Corn Exchange building, with one hand for Bristol time and one for London time.

When the line from Bristol to Exeter was extended to Plymouth, for instance, the railways had to overcome a time difference of 17 minutes. The answer, in Bristol and Bath at least, was imaginative, if not plain weird. The council simply added an extra minute hand to the Corn Exchange clock so it showed both Bristol and London time. The clock itself dates back to 1819 and was made by Thwaites and Reede. It operates by a series of weights and pulleys and still has to be wound up every Saturday morning. The three hands idea was well meant, but as every other clock in Bristol showed local time only, the public remained totally confused. You can see why yourself by trying to read the right time today. At least Bristol tried to tackle the problem unlike some other towns and cities – the people of Exeter, for example, refused outright to accept GMT, which they called 'Cockney time'. However it wasn't the railways that led to the adoption of national time: it was the electric telegraph. By 1851, when a telegraph opened between London and Bristol, Britain was becoming too small for different time zones. As historian John Latimer recorded ponderously: 'The rapid development of telegraphic business brought into increased prominence the troublesome question of local time still registered by the parish clocks, messages from London being received at Bristol about 10 minutes before… they purported to be dispatched'. In 1852, the City Corporation finally agreed to adopt Greenwich time, but it wasn't until 1880 that Parliament finally ordered the whole country to do so. International time zones, based on Greenwich as a base line, followed four years later as did British summer time in 1916 as part of an effort to increase productivity during the war. That's still with us, despite many efforts to get rid of it. At some time, the extra minute hand on the Corn Exchange clock was removed and forgotten until 1983 when the clock was being restored, and the stub of the extra hand was rediscovered. Bristol clock engineer Andy Nicholls made a new hand to match the original and the refurbished clock was reinstalled in 1989. Once again, this unique piece of Bristoliana is baffling people who just want to know the time. Under Lord Archer's plan, England would be on European mainland time while Scotland would keep current hours. This would give England an extra hour's daylight in the evenings, and, says Lord Archer, cut crime and accidents. Tell that to the Victorian train traveller!

I came, I saw, I conkered

How do you become the 'conkerer' of the neighbourhood when the horse chestnuts begin to fall?

Scientists across the world have been studying this question and they have divided conker players into three categories – those who bake, those who soak and those who prefer their weapons to mature and mellow with age. The Bakers are not approved of in some circles although in a game with few rules, it's hard to break them. This method does give your conker a crisp hardness that can shatter the opposition, although over-baking can make it brittle. The Soakers: everyone has their own secret recipe for pickling conkers to an iron consistency. Vinegar is the usual choice, but paraffin or even urine are recommended by some champion players. However, there is an alternative – dunking them in Oil of Olay. This apparently has the effect of making them soft and supple and able to absorb the impact of a pickled conker – doesn't do much for its own striking power, though. The Agers: nothing beats the sheer, rock hard brutality of the OAP conker, lovingly stored for half a century or so. One of these venerable nuts will see off any number of pretentious young whipper-snappers. Lay some down for your grandchildren now.

Girls just want to have fun. Conkers seems to have come back into fashion lately, but as more of an adult pub game rather than for kids. Like lots of other traditional games it has been banned from many schools on safety grounds.

The game of conkers is rarely found outside Britain except in British colonies with either horse chestnut trees or with someone at home willing to export nuts each autumn.

It's a brutal world, too. At the national conker championships in Poulton, near Cirencester, contestants were searched to ensure they weren't carrying hardened conkers to substitute for their official entries. Vinegared conkers are out, and all entries are examined, drilled and stringed by the committee. 'I have known grown men get very upset if they lose,' says organizer Kevin McIntyre. 'I once had to ban a vet from the contest for the unforgivable sin of hitting me over the head with a conker.'

Bristol 600

In 1973, Bristol marked the end of 600 years as a city and county with a huge festival on the Downs.

It started off as a massive celebration of 600 years of the city and county of Bristol. It ended in a mud-bath, the collapse of the organizing company and the disappearance of one of the directors. But it was a great idea and it was fun. And only the weather stopped it being the biggest and best show the West has ever seen – until the amazing Festival of the Sea in 1996, that is.

Bristol has now regained its independence as a city and county.

In 1973, it was glumly resigned to losing the title, which it had held for 600 years, and becoming part of the new county of Avon. But it was decided to go out with a bang, and the Bristol 600 Exhibition was born. It was held on the Downs, backed by the *Evening Post* and run by a company called Commerce Displays, whose promotions director was one Eric Castle.

The programme was ambitious to say the least – 'the biggest and most spectacular ever staged in the city', according to the council. Apart from the exhibition, there were plans for five miles of strip lighting along Portway; floodlighting of Queen Square, Brandon Hill and the Centre; 600 new trees, and flags and flowers everywhere. Centrepiece of the show was a Medieval Fayre complete with a reconstruction of Bristol Castle, ox-roasting, nightly banquets and some very exciting jousting that produced one or two very real injuries. Most big Bristol companies like Harveys, Rolls-Royce and BAC had their own pavilions and there was a 1,000-seat theatre with a continuous programme of entertainment from cooking and concerts to beauty and talent contests. The BBC joined in by staging the international final of *Jeux Sans Frontiers* ('It's a Knockout', Euro-style) and transmitting it to 400 million viewers. And there were all kinds of martial displays, a working Great Western Railway steam locomotive, and much, much more.

The jamboree lasted from July 21 to August 21 – and it was nearly washed out before it opened. Torrential rain and gale-force winds wrecked several marquees and nearly destroyed the unique Bristol Tapestry. Tons of straw and chippings were laid as the mud grew deeper, and wellies were the order of the day. A brief spell of good weather boosted attendances before more heavy rain reduced the show to a shambles. The final blow was when the Queen decided to give the exhibition a miss because of the mud. There were massive protests, especially from traders and exhibitors, who had made every effort to keep the sodden show going.

The Palace finally relented and the Queen did turn up – very late and riding on the back of a Land Rover. She stayed for less than 20 minutes and had a less than enthusiastic welcome.

Medieval fun. Just one of the crazy stunts that made up the Bristol 600 celebrations on the Downs.

The show was great entertainment and the few days of good weather showed what tremendous potential it had. But when it was over, Commerce Displays went bust and Eric Castle disappeared to South Africa at the same time that £73,000 takings vanished. In 1979, he was killed in Rhodesia (now Zimbabwe) in a rocket attack during the revolution, ending plans to extradite him.

But tens of thousands of people enjoyed the show, despite the weather. It was a good way to sign off 600 years of history – but with good weather, it would have been a great one.

The plant hunters

If it wasn't for men like Joseph Banks, Robert Fortune and Ernest Wilson risking death, torture and amorous native queens, British gardens might be very different.

Few people realize that familiar plants like rhododendron, winter-flowering jasmine, gladioli and honeysuckle were brought to Britain after epic adventures in remote corners of the world.

When you sip a soothing cuppa, remember that India's tea industry might never have been, without an intrepid plant smuggler who brought bushes out of the far reaches of China.

To give Britain the lobelia, Francis Masson had to fight off pirates and the French, while introducing the rhododendron nearly cost George Forrest his life at the hands of bloodthirsty Tibetan lamas. Discovering many species of pines and spruces put David Douglas up against Indians and grizzly bears which he survived, only to be gored to death by a bull in Hawaii.

Joseph Hooker – who brought back 6,000 Himalayan species – found himself used as an excuse for the British to march into the little kingdom of Sikkim and add it to the Empire.

Robert Fortune, the man who launched the Indian tea industry, was typical of the breed. He was sent to China in 1843 at a time when foreigners were hated and faced numerous attacks by hostile villagers. He suffered storms at sea, attacks by pirates, muggings and a narrow escape from death in a boar pit. In the true tradition of Victorian adventurers, he shaved his head, attached a false pigtail and wore Chinese clothes to visit the forbidden city of Soochow. Among the many plants he introduced to Britain were varieties of japonica, anemone, forsythia, jasmine, weigela, mahonia and rhododendron. But his biggest contribution to horticultural history was the establishment of the Indian tea industry. He toured remote parts of China and illegally sent 23,892 plants, 17,000 seedlings and eight Chinese

Plant hunter. Robert Fortune, the explorer who went to China, found many unusual species and launched the Indian tea industry.

growers to the foothills of the Himalayas. Plantations were set up in Assam and Sikkim and tea soon became a major Indian export. Fortune was also hired by the United States government to set up a tea industry in America, and 32,000 plants were grown before the Civil War ruined the plans.

The fascinating story of Fortune's exploits was told in great detail in *The Plant Hunters*, a remarkable collection of tales of derring-do, exploration and wild adventure by *Evening Post* gardening expert Toby Musgrave, his archaeologist brother Will and his business partner Chris Gardner. They concentrated on 10 of the most important plant hunters, from Joseph Banks who travelled with Captain Cook and established the supremacy of Kew Gardens, to Frank Kingdom Ward who found the stunning blue Himalayan poppy. The impact on ordinary British gardens of these men is considerable and the efforts they went to get them quite overwhelming.

Joseph Banks introduced more than 7,000 new species from South America and the Pacific, smuggled merino sheep from Spain to Australia and fought off a nymphomaniac Tahitian queen. Francis Masson faced poisonous snakes, hurricanes and French pirates to give Britain the beautiful amaryllis belladonna lily, the gladioli and the lobelia. Ernest Wilson suffered starvation, a train wreck, crippling injury and arrest for spying to bring back the first giant panda seen in the West, and varieties of clematis, acer, davidia, viburnum, regal lily, primula, cornus, magnolia and thousands of other bulbs, shrubs and herbaceous species.

Perhaps Frank Kingdon-Ward's 100 new rhododendron species might not be appreciated these days in areas like Exmoor where the hardy plants are killing off all other plant life, and there's no tribute in this book to the importers of pests like Japanese knotweed and Russian vine. But as the

Easter adventure. Chinese junks similar to those on which Fortune travelled when he was attacked by pirates.

Musgraves and Chris Gardner say: 'The plant hunters were exceptional men who dedicated their lives to increasing the understanding of botany and horticulture. Between them, they collected tens of thousands of new species and gardeners around the world owe them an enormous debt'.

Private Harrison, D. – war criminal

The time has come to confess. I am guilty of a war crime, [writes the author].

After 40 years, I feel I should ease my conscience and admit that I took part in chemical warfare of a kind banned by the Geneva Convention. It all happened because my friend Clive and I were fed up to the back teeth with the relentless grind of studying for A-levels. Youth clubs were beginning to pall – so we joined the Territorial Army. I think it was more because we were more impressed with Clive's uncle, who sparkled in gilt and braid as some sort of sergeant major, than we were interested in serving our country. Anyway, it all sounded great fun, so, at the age of 17, I became a weekend trooper in the 44th Tank Regiment/North Somerset Yeomanry based at Keynsham.

Lord knows why I did it. I hate regimentation and being told what to do, and the whole army ethos offended my newly-developed sense of independence.

We were kitted out in dreadful uniforms with ludicrous gaiters into which trouser legs were stuffed and carefully spread to hang in required army fashion. I had a stylish beret perched on my bushy hair (we strongly resisted army haircuts) and looked a veritable picture of martial ferocity.

I've never experienced anything quite as bizarre as the Terriers. I never could get the hang (or the point) of marching up and down, crashing mirror bright boots on the floor and turning smartly on the spot. Eventually the drill sergeant more or less gave up.

We had a fleet of little armoured cars – Ferrets – with Rolls-Royce engines carefully sealed away from prying fingers and only serviceable by a Rolls-Royce engineer with a key. I often wondered how many of them would be lurking on a battlefield if you blew a gasket?

I couldn't drive, so when we went out in them I sat on the open upper seat above the hidden driver, basking in the admiration and envy of the peasantry as we thundered down the A37.

I was officially a radio operator – although I was better at tuning in to Radio Luxembourg than HQ – but, as juniors, Clive and I were also general dogsbodies. We had our moments though. We went for live gunnery practice to the range at Pilning when it was our job to load the magazines for some kind of machine gun. We were promised a go on the trigger if we behaved ourselves, so we carefully filled each magazine with the requisite number of rounds and watched enviously as our colleagues played Rambo. Finally it was our turn. We quietly crammed our magazines as full of bullets as they would take – far more than allowed by regulations – and set the guns on automatic.

It was like using a hosepipe. A stream of bullets sprayed across the range, not only hitting the wooden targets but completely chewing them up into little fragments. It was a spectacular sight and one well worth the lecture that followed.

Then there was the great Quantocks adventure. We were divided into groups, covered our faces with boot polish and were dropped off in the wilds in the dead of night with just a compass, a torch and a map. The aim was to get back to our farm HQ for cocoa and bed. It was very cold, and as dark as it only can be in the country. And apart from the natural hazards, there were officers scattered around the area shooting flares at anything that moved.

We got our map upside down and headed off in the wrong direction from the start. We were miserable, hungry and tired and beginning to wish we'd stuck with the youth club when we heard a strange noise behind us. The corporal allegedly commanding our commando outfit risked a flash of his torch, and the beam reflected off a semi-circle of glaring red eyes which, with a noise out of hell, began to move rapidly towards us.

With the true British grit that has served the Tommy through the ages, we ran – or tried to. Unfortunately, we hadn't realized we were on the edge of a river and most of our troop went straight in. I hung on to a passing tree as what turned out to be a herd of deer, headed by an angry stag (it was the rutting season) charged past. As most of us were now cold, hungry, tired and wet as well, we gave up and called for help from the first phone box we found. No medals that evening.

And the chemical warfare? Well, the best fun we had in the Terriers was when we were allowed to play with tanks on Salisbury Plain. On this occasion, we were teamed up with the Somerset Light Infantry who were invaders trying to get past our defensive tank line. To my horror, as they were a bit short that day, I was delegated to abandon my tank and become a foot soldier. Oh, the humiliation! They were very keen, the SLI. One chap even went as far as hiding himself in the middle of a steaming compost heap to avoid being spotted. My group were trapped in a wooded copse with one of those lovely tanks rumbling menacingly below. That was

War criminal: David Harrison, self-confessed chemical warfare enthusiast, in captivity by his father's greenhouse.

when we came up with a cunning plan. The SLI also had some schoolboys playing at soldiering like me and one had some stink bombs. He took off his boots, very quietly climbed onto the tank and rolled his stinkers down the barrel. When the crew shot through the hatch coughing and spluttering, we had them surrounded. With those magical military words 'Bang, you're dead!' we had captured a tank – a feat never achieved before. Sadly, we were disqualified. We got a pat on the back for initiative but were lectured on Britain's obligations under the Geneva Convention and warned that chemical warfare was illegal. Still, we did it, and in my book, all's fair in love and war!

Territorials Fact File

For centuries, England had bands of yeomanry and militia formed by feudal lords and local squires who were called up in times of war and civil unrest. In the early days, regiments were named after the colonel who clothed and paid for the men (and often made a profit) and who could buy and sell the unit. The Gloucestershire Regiment was named Gibson's, de Lalo's, Mordaunt's and Bragg's before becoming the 28th Foot. By 1803, a volunteer army of some 400,000 was prepared to defend the country against a French invasion. They were poorly trained and scarcely equipped at all, and were disbanded when the threat from Napoleon ended. The part-timers were called up whenever problems arose at home or abroad, but the Boer war made it obvious that untrained volunteers were no longer adequate for modern warfare.

In 1907, the War Minister, Lord Haldane, combined the militia, yeomanry and volunteers as the Territorial Army – immediately nicknamed Haldane's Horse. It was mainly there for home defence but could volunteer for overseas service.

By 1939, the TA had 250,000 members with a corps for women called the Auxiliary Territorial Service. It was incorporated into the regular army during the Second World War, but cut back to 150,000 troops in 1946. Numbers were increased to 300,000 in 1956, and the TA was described as 'a vital force of national necessity.' This made a pleasant change from derisory nicknames like the Featherbed Heroes, the Dog Shooters or the Saturday Night Soldiers.

Keynsham Co-op

Keynhsam Co-op was a Victorian dream that turned into a nightmare. However it very nearly worked, despite some rather dubious practices.

Keynsham's very own Co-op started on Bedminster railway station. It bumbled through the problems of bacon curing, dubious sales techniques and fraud, and lasted just 11 years. It was a classic example of the small village Co-op, set up to benefit members but not really big enough to survive on its own.

It was in 1894 that a group of Keynsham villagers were so inspired by the enthusiasm of the Bedminster Co-operators that they decided to set up their own. They became so excited by the prospect they each handed over a shilling to Mr T.R. Tucker, who volunteered to be treasurer while waiting for the train home one day. A public meeting was called a week later and attracted around 40 people. A committee was set up and on November 23, 1894, Keynsham Co-operative opened its first shop with a tea party for Bedminster, Bristol and Gloucester friends who gave 'inspiring addresses to these young beginners in Co-operation'.

The first (and only) store was away from the rest of the village shops (Keynsham was still a village then) and with nothing, apart from a meagre window display, to distinguish it from other cottages in the road. It was very much an amateur business. Mr T.J. Harvey, Co-op secretary, his wife and daughter ran the store in addition to their newspaper and magazine distribution service.

President Bill Harris, a milkman, provided milk at a discount, allowed members to share in the profits, and even fetched goods for sale from Bristol himself to help cut costs. But the lack of professionalism did have unfortunate side effects. The Co-operators started curing their own bacon but treated too much at once and couldn't sell it fast enough. In a hot summer, it went off.

'A council of ways and means was called to seal the fate of some hundredweights of their home cured which ended in a pilgrimage to the back garden, and there the unsavoury meats were consigned to Mother Earth' says a 1911 history of the society. After that, Keynsham gave up bacon curing and bought ready-cured meat from Trowbridge Co-operators.

However Keynsham wasn't above a bit of sharp practice. A member who was also a grocer persuaded the shop to put a box of 4d

T. GODFREY. W. HARRIS. J. WILLIAMS.

E. FRANKHAM. J. CHARD.

J. G. HARVEY. G. BEES. F. BRYANT.

Victorian pioneers. The men who founded the Keynsham Co-op in 1894.

currants on sale for 5d. The first person to get caught by the scam was the grocer's wife.

'This was the first and last attempt to copy the methods of the smart trader' says the history ruefully. Surprisingly, the Co-operators only made a loss once – and that was due to a shop assistant decamping with the £14 from the till.

Keynsham was a small society that didn't try to sell itself. Membership hovered around the 62 mark and there was an arrangement with a local baker and butcher for members to buy bread and meat at a discount, using tokens bought from the Co-operators. It couldn't last. Keynsham was surrounded by larger and more prosperous co-ops at Bedminster, East Twerton and Radstock which paid bigger dividends, and the new tramway system opened up the shops of Bristol and Bath to Keynsham shoppers. In 1896, and against the wishes of the Co-op founders, it was decided to seek amalgamation with Bedminster. To everyone's surprise, Bedminster turned down the idea, and Keynsham was left to struggle on its own. Then in 1904, Ethel Harvey, who was managing the shop, moved to a co-op in Oxfordshire. Talks with Bedminster were reopened and in 1905, the two societies finally merged. Both were immediately swallowed up by the new Bristol Co-operative Society Ltd.

Bristol Slasher

Was the Bristol Slasher really a war hero – or was he a fraud?

Jemmy Phillips, alias the 'Bristol Slasher', has lain with honour in St Mary Redcliffe churchyard for 177 years. He was a remarkable Indiana Jones-style hero who fought with Nelson at Trafalgar. Or at least that's what he claimed. If research by Nelson Society member Martin Telling is anything to go by, Phillips may have been one of Bristol's cleverest conmen.

Reports in Bristol newspapers from 1818 tell of Phillips' bravery as Nelson's boatswain on board *Victory*. Martin has also found a long account in the *Western Daily Press* of 1908 by an anonymous writer whose father knew Phillips well. The story was astonishing. Phillips, a Bedminster man, was stationed on *Victory*'s forecastle and a painting of the battle at Greenwich does indeed show a figure which acquaintances reckoned was 'a capital likeness' of Jemmy.

'During that engagement, he received four large sabre cuts on his head, many gunshot wounds in the body and three balls in his right thigh and leg,' claims the writer. 'He was attacked by three French sailors at once. One he killed and the other two he forced overboard.' The author of the piece also quotes a letter from an unnamed midshipman on the *Victory* which states:

'In the great heat of the battle, the Bristol Slasher had been killed twice but it appears he came to life again. He appeared, according to the statements of some of the men with him, to have been the special man aimed at on the bows of our ship.'

The nickname was allegedly given to him by an admiring Nelson. The midshipman's letter says the Bristol Slasher was 'so damaged in the terrific fight that he came back to Bedminster where he resided until his death.'

Jemmy Phillips lived in honour in North Street, where he reportedly assisted Bristol Poet Laureate and historian Robert Southey in writing an account of the battle. He was apparently given several mementos of Nelson by the admiral's descendant, Revd William Nelson. They included a cigar case given to Nelson by Lady Hamilton, a tobacco cutter made from a captured French gun, and teak from a French ship. In 1908, the *Western Daily Press* reported that these items were still owned by a Bristol family.

On March 9, 1819, the Bristol Slasher was 'boarded by the grim tyrant Death' and 'this brave tar's remains were towed to their last moorings in the churchyard of St Mary Redcliffe.' Jemmy Phillips does indeed have an impressive tomb in the churchyard. Sadly, however, it seems none of his story was true: 'Having spoken to every possible source, it appears that the Bristol Slasher was, indeed, the Bristol Bluffer,' said Martin.

'That he was boatswain is untrue, as is his service on *Victory*. That he was at Trafalgar is highly improbable and he definitely was not acquainted with Nelson. There are so many various records of those who served with Nelson and indeed in the Royal Navy in general. Mr Phillips does not appear anywhere in those records. Revd William Nelson was a particularly mean and selfish man who allowed Lady Hamilton to die in poverty in Calais. For him to give anything away was extremely rare. Robert Southey had sources from Lady Fanny Nelson to the officers of Victory and friends of Nelson, and would not need to speak to anyone of lowly rank.

'I believe Jemmy Phillips' greatest feat was to hide his secret for 177 years.'

Fraudster. Jemmy Phillips' ornate tomb in St Mary Redcliffe churchyard.

Sea battle. Had Jemmy Phillips been on board the Victory *with Nelson at the battle of Trafalgar, or was he just a barefaced liar?*

Bishopston

Bishopston is today a peaceful residential suburb off the Gloucester Road. But it began with an argument that had to be settled by Parliament.

Bishopston today seems little different from Redland and St Andrews which borders it to the east and west. The houses are a little younger than old Redland, and a little older than most of St Andrews. But it took Parliament to settle an argument which held up the development of the land for years. In the 1840s, the area where Berkeley and Egerton Roads now stand was farmland and orchards in the countryside between Bristol and Horfield, which was said to be so wild that a small Horfield boy froze to death on his way home one night.

It was obviously prime building land once Cotham and Montpelier were built up, but it was then part of the manor of Horfield over which the Bishop of Gloucester and Bristol had virtually feudal rights. The Ecclesiastical Commissioners decided in 1846 to take over the lease of Horfield – then a much different parish than today – on the grounds that the income topped the £5,000 a year permitted.

The bishop, Dr James Monk (remembered in Bishop Road and Monk Road among others) offered to sell his interests for £11,587, with half the proceeds going to his family and half towards improving the living of poor parsons. Dr Monk managed to negotiate a lease which would have given him the title Lord Farmer as well as the recipient of that useful £545 a year. The complexity of the situation and the ancient feudal rights led to debates in Parliament, with doubts over the legal status of the bishop's holdings as well as the rights of leaseholders and copy-holders on the estate. While this was going on, no development could take place. Dr Monk seems to have been a well-meaning man who tried to thread his way through the ancient Laws of lease and copy-holding as best he could. But the £545 a year income from the manor attracted the interest of the Revd Henry Richards, Perpetual Curate of Horfield (an old title

Tree lined. The handsome, well-built houses of Bishopston have been popular with home-buyers since the area was developed in Victorian times.

with feudal powers), who tried to persuade Parliament that Dr Monk had no right to sell the lease. Richards, the largest copy-holder, had an eye on the cash and the title, and was furious at the bishop trying to strike a deal without his agreement. As Dr Monk recorded, 'His indignation exhibited itself in railing against his bishop'.

In the end the government vetoed the deal, so Dr Monk granted a new lease 'for three lives' to his secretary. Parliament was very unhappy with the compromise, with MPs insisting the bishop should have regarded the manor as a public trust rather than his own property.

Dr Monk argued that he wanted to end the ancient feudal rights system and improve the living of Horfield and this was the best way to do it. The row simmered on until 1858 when a board of trustees finally bought the lease for £5,000. 'With the emancipation of the district from the copy-hold system dates its rise and rapid growth as a suburb' recorded annalist John Latimer.

But the greedy Richards was not finished. He agreed to the formation of a new parish in Horfield to be called Bishopston and for the bishop to be the patron. But after Dr Monks' death, he backed down, claiming he would never allow a Low churchman to nominate a clergyman in his parish. Richards obviously had his eye on the value of living, which was increasing as Bishopston developed. He built a new church on Gloucester Road and offered to endow it, providing the patronage was vested in him and his heirs. But the trustees now administering the manor of Horfield persuaded the new bishop to once again reject Richard's offer 'to the great wrath of the vicar who must have seen that through the increasing population, the value of the living would soon be augmented'. The church of St Michael and All Angels was opened on June 20, 1858 on what is locally still called Pigsty Hill. The new parish included parts of Horfield, Stapleton and Montpelier parishes. Bishopston, the suburb, began with Berkeley and Egerton roads, handsome tree-lined streets built in orchards stocked with mature trees, many of which still survive today.

There is a persistent story handed down in the area that no pairs of houses were to be identical. It is impossible to say if it is true after more than a century, but there is still an astonishing diversity in house design and decoration.

Richards reappeared in history one more time when he opened a pleasure garden at Horfield on the lines of Rennison's in Montpelier. However, it was too far out of town for fashionable Bristolians and it soon closed. Richard cut his losses by selling the land to Bristol Corporation for a new prison which is still there today. Sadly, his church of St Michael's, a local landmark for more than a century, had to be demolished in the 1990s when it was found to be unsafe.

Brislington House

There is a 150 year-old link between Brislington, Bristol and the City of the Eels in Australia.

Brislington House was built in 1821, and for nearly a century housed the Brown family of doctors. However, even older Bristolians would have problems recognizing it because it stands in Parramatta, New South Wales, Australia. Yet there is a strong link with Bristol's Brislington and Keynsham and that part of Australia, as former Bristolian Bill Cridland discovered on a visit.

The house was built for one John Hodge, a prisoner who had been transported to New South Wales in 1806. He tried to escape by stowing away on a whaler, but was recaptured, so he settled down-under with a wife and children and began a life of petty crime. He managed to win his freedom with a rather dubious venture involving horse and cart hire, and ran a very successful illicit grog business. Then he won £1,000 in gold at cards, bought some land and started building the house. As the eight of diamonds had been his winning card, he had an eight of diamonds design picked out in brickwork on a back wall. However Hodge had to sell the house when he was jailed for a year for illegally selling drink. It was then discovered that his kitchen fireplace had been made from a stolen mortuary stone (the slab later became a garden seat).

The house was sold in 1825 together with one of the first five wells dug in Australia. By 1857, it was occupied by Dr Walter Brown who named it Brislington after the (then) Somerset village in which he was born in 1821. He was one of nine children of architect John Brown and his wife Mary. His mother died when he was 10 but he was well educated by his father. When he was 16 he was apprenticed to Bristol surgeon I.G. Lansdown before training further at Edinburgh University. He became a General Practitioner in Keynsham before emigrating to New South Wales where he settled in Parramatta (Aborigine for 'City of the Eels').

When British troops withdrew from the colony, the Parramatta Volunteer Rifle Corps was founded with Dr Brown as captain. Every evening the corps marched down the main street from the government house to assemble outside Brislington where the union flag was lowered at sunset.

Dr Brown was also a strong force behind the development of hospital facilities in the settlement after having to remove an ovarian cyst from a patient in a local boarding house. By the time he died in 1897, a new hospital

Long Fox Manor: Now luxury flats and re-maned after a Georgian pioneer in psychiatric treatment, the old Brislington House is more warmly remembered as a home for nurses.

Brislington House. The home of the Brown family in Parramatta, New South Wales.

was under construction. His son, Walter Sigismund, took over Brislington and the practice in 1889, and his grandson, Keith, followed in 1919. But in 1947, the hospital decided to take over Brislington as a nurses' home and Dr Keith moved to a nearby street until his death in 1962.

Brislington had been a family home and medical practice for 92 years, and today houses a collection of medical and nursing memorabilia. It also holds some pictures of Bristol's Brislington. Bill Cridland, who lived in Be-I-Bristol, Yennora, New South Wales, comments, 'I took a book along showing some pictures of Brislington old and new, which they copied, so they may find a space there somewhere. As Walter Brown was one of five children, it is likely that there are still members of the family still living in Bristol'.

Almshouses

Almshouses have been a refuge for the poor and sick for a thousand years and are still being built today.

You'll find them scattered around Bristol and Avon's villages – buildings preserving a remarkable unbroken tradition of more than 1,000 years. Some are homes for dozens of old folk – others for just two or three. Some are run by trusts, others by churches or charities. But all are almshouses.

They were Britain's first sheltered accommodation – a refuge for the helpless in the days when poverty could mean death, and even though the Welfare State provides a safety net today, almshouses are still flourishing. Bristol has some of the most picturesque, for example the timbered splendours of John Foster's at the top of Christmas Steps, the unexpected tranquillity of Barstaple's on the corner of Old Market and Midland Road and the quiet oasis of Merchant Seamen's at the end of King Street, dismally overshadowed by office blocks.

Barstaple House, with 31 flats, beautifully-carved timber work and an elegant garden, is a little- known haven of peace in frantic Old Market, but both it and John Foster's are said to be outdated and in need of replacement. Few people realize that almshouses are still being built, and among the most recent are Perrett's House, Redcross Street, and Bethany Home in Bedminster.

Almshouses descended from hospitals – places offering hospitality – which cared for the old and sick, as well as poor travellers. The meaning of 'hospital' has changed, of course, and that can cause problems – Trinity Hospital almshouse in Old Market had to change its name after passers-by kept calling in to seek medical attention. Most were originally set up by religious houses or wealthy benefactors who gave cash or the income from land to provide the needy with a home, food and a small pension. There are more than 30 groups of almshouses in the area and many have a fascinating history.

Crispe's at Marshfield was built by the Crispe family between 1612 and 1625. Its income comes from London rents, money left by the family, and a local field. Thomas Gully left £100 in 1890 to build cottages for Longwell Green residents. They are still there today.

Foster's, above Christmas Steps, was founded by salt merchant John Foster between 1481-1484 (he lived in what is now Foster's Rooms in Small Street) and was expanded by Henry VIII's doctor. It includes the only chapel in England dedicated to the Three Kings of Cologne, the three wise men who visited the infant Jesus, but most of the almshouse was rebuilt between 1860 and 1880.

Residents of Dr White's, now rebuilt in Redcliffe, were treated to a 'pease and pork dinner' every December 21.

Colston's on St Michael's Hill was built in 1691 by merchant Edward Colston for £2,500 for 12 elderly men and 12 elderly women who

Three kings. Statues of the Three Kings of Cologne (the three wise men) grace the fine buildings which make up Fosters almshouse at the top of Christmas Steps.

Old salts. The Merchant Seamans almshouses at the end of King Street, where many an old sailor has ended his days in peace and quiet.

Almshouse. Trininy Hospital South, on the busy corner of Midland Road and Old Market was founded by John Barstaple in 1395.

were both Bristolian and regular Church of England attendees. The almshouse has its own chapel, walled in old ship's timbers, and residents were rounded up each morning and made to attend. The rules were later relaxed, making chapel compulsory only three times a week and then weekly.

Most almshouses have been modernized to make very pleasant flats for the elderly and residents.

Acceptance into an almshouse depends on who runs it, and the terms of the original endowment, but most take people recommended by doctors, welfare agencies or the Church. Different charities have different requirements according to their charters – some take anyone between 55 and 80 who are homeless, overcrowded, or simply vulnerable, while others demand a link with a specific church or organization.

Almshouses Fact File:
• 'Alms' comes from the Latin *eleemosina*, meaning gifts to the poor.
• To 'live on the alms basket' meant to live on charity.
• An 'alms-drink' referred to dregs which a drinker couldn't finish and handed to someone else.
• There are 2,358 groups of almshouses in Britain – 35,000 dwellings in all.
• The oldest surviving almshouses are in Canterbury, Norwich and Winchester. The earliest recorded was in York in AD 965.
• Nearly 1,000 groups of almshouses offer between one and five dwellings and 1,320 have between six and 50. Only 51 have more than 50.

Repairs. Many almshouses are very ancient and in constant need of costly repairs.

Refuge. Almshouses like these provided the only safe haven for the elderly poor in days gone by.

Stately mansion. The imposing South front of Ashton Court. There has been a house on this site since medieval times.

Ashton Court

Plans for a £4.5 million restoration of Ashton Court estate, one of the West's largest public parks, won the backing of the Heritage Lottery Fund.

The history of Ashton Court has been inextricably linked with Bristol since its beginnings. People have lived on what is now the estate since at least the Iron Age and possibly before, and field patterns still exist dating back to the days when the Romans had a villa there.

Part of the Wansdyke, an ancient fortification running from Portishead to Andover, passed through Long Ashton, but it was the Normans who laid the foundations of the modern estate.

Ashton (originating from the Saxon 'Estune') became the property of the Warrior Bishop of Coutances who built the first Bristol castle. It passed to Robert de Mowbray, his nephew, who lost it in an ill-conceived rebellion against the king in 1095. The land passed through several owners until it was sold to William de Lyons (William of Ashton) at the end of the thirteenth century. When William died in 1312, he left a house, Ashton Court, on 147 acres of arable land with 44 acres of meadow, numerous fields and three mills. The estate stayed in the hands of the de Lyons and in 1392, Thomas de Lyons enclosed and planted the magnificent park, as well as building Long Ashton church (his Arms are engraved on the tower). Thomas was also granted the right of Free Warren –

Twenties' luxury. The Long Gallery at Ashton Court, pictured in 1929 when the Smyth family were in residence.

that is to hunt game – and he set up a seven-acre conygre, or rabbit warren, in the grounds. He also married Bristol heiress Margaret Blanket, one of the family which popularized the woollen bed covering.

Ashton Court passed through the hands of a number of important owners, including Sir Richard Choke of Stanton Drew, the Chief Justice; Lord Daubney, King's Chamberlain; and Sir Thomas Arundel, one of Henry VIIIs commissioners for suppressing religious houses, who was later beheaded for rebellion. Before his death, he sold the mansion to Bristol merchant John Smyth.

The rest of the history of Ashton Court concerns the Smyth family who lived there for four centuries until the death of the Honourable Mrs Esme Smyth in 1946. John Smyth was sheriff and twice mayor of Bristol, but his son, Hugh, was a wild character involved in poaching, armed robbery and assaults, and who was only saved from jail or

execution by the regular payment of heavy fines. But it was Hugh who enlarged the park with his mother – a trend followed by three succeeding generations who expanded further to create the huge estate seen today.

His son, Thomas, who was MP for Bridgwater, helped raise money to have St Paul's Cathedral repaired after the Fire of London and was one of the last of the great estate owners to keep a resident jester (his name was Austin). Thomas became a Royalist commander in the Civil War and King Charles II made his son a baronet and personally stayed at the mansion.

It was during the seventeenth century that the formal garden was built and a new south-west wing added in the style of the Inigo Jones banqueting hall in Whitehall.

The top designer of the day, Humphrey Repton, who also designed Blaise estate, was called in 1802 and was thrilled with the view of busy Bristol and its river from the estate.

Family organ. The Music Room in the '20s. It even had its own organ, now sadly lost along with the fine furniture.

Some of his ideas were used in the planting of the estate and its drives. The five mile long park wall was completed around 1804 and 10,000 new trees and 750 shrubs planted. Deer were added from 1830 onwards.

The male line of Smyths had died out but various descendants adopted the name by Royal Warrant, including lawyer, slave trader and coal baron Jarit Smyth (born Smith) and Sir Greville Smyth (born Upton). It was during his time at Ashton Court that one Tom Provis tried to take advantage of the convoluted family history by claiming to be Sir Richard Smyth. He was exposed and died in prison.

Sir Greville continued the planting and brought in trees from America, including very unsuitable giant Californian sequoias. He died in 1901 and the Smyth male line was again extinct. Once again, the new house owner took on the Smyth name and Esme Irby became the Hon. Mrs Esme Smyth.

When Mrs Smyth died in 1946, the days of the mansion as a family home died with her. Like so many great country houses, it had been deteriorating since the First World War, and the city council decided to buy it. But the Second World War broke out and the house was requisitioned by the army, although Mrs Smyth remained living there.

The council finally bought the house in 1959 and although the park is a firm family favourite, it has been looking for ways to do something with the house ever since. The improvement programme includes restoring the landscape and formal gardens, adding a new visitor centre, extending a café, refurbishing the estate buildings, and improving the golf course and deer park.

The estate is visited by more than 1.5 million people a year, and has hosted some of the West's biggest and most popular events, including the North Somerset Show, the International Balloon Fiesta, the kite festival and Community Festival.

The Blue Danube. Looking more like a dirty ditch than a waterway, this is the River Frome where it enters the heart of the city. Locals nicknamed it the Danny – but why?

The Danny

Why is there a river in Bristol known as the Danny? Exhaustive inquiries have failed to find out.

The Danny has seen plenty of changes in the thousand of years or so that Bristol has existed. If you know what the Danny is, chances are you live near it as it flows through central and east Bristol. To everyone else, it's known as the River Frome.

Bristol was built where the Frome (formerly the Froom) meets the Avon. There were marshes there that, over the centuries, were drained and it was the Frome that was dug out and straightened to form the astonishing St Augustine's Trench, now buried beneath The Centre.

The Danny runs beneath Penn Street – named for William Penn, the Quaker slave owner who founded Pennsylvania – from River Street. Until it was covered at the turn of the last century, the River Street stretch was a favourite spot for children to fish and paddle. It was also an occasional enemy for heavy rains led the water to rise and flood the surrounding areas.

The Danny comes in beneath Wade Street, named after Major Nathaniel Wade who was wounded fighting for the Duke of Monmouth. The bridge over the Frome in Wade Street was long known as Traitor's Bridge because Wade backed the wrong side, but he was pardoned, witnessed William Penn's marriage and became Town Clerk of Bristol. The river reaches Wade Street along Wellington Road, named after the victor at Waterloo. And, like the wall around New Street Flats in River Street, the culvert here is partly built from the hard slag left by the copper and brass industries of Bristol.

On the other side of Easton Way, the river runs beneath Baptist Mills, which was probably where the Roman Via Julia, from Sea Mills to Bath, crossed. Baptist, incidentally, has nothing to do with the church – it is thought to be derived from a local family of mill owners called Bagpath, or a cloth made there called baptiste.

It was here that the Bristol Brass Wire Company, the most important in Europe, was established and waste-slag was used in the walls of the Greek church there.

Baptist Mills was also the site of White's Pottery where Egyptian Black teapots were made and the White brothers jealously guarded the secret process for making green and yellow Mr Punch pipes. Pottery and mill were demolished in the nineteenth century so the river could be widened and deepened to stop flooding.

Near to the river course is the Old Fox, where W.G. Grace drank when he lived in Stapleton Road and was a doctor in Easton. Close by is the Black Swan, an impressive Grade II listed building and once the home of Bristol Rovers, bottlers F.W. Hunt and two coach companies.

Before that, the Danny passes what was once the Rover ground (which often flooded until 1968) and is now a shopping centre. Earlier, it runs into Eastville Park, built as a work-creation scheme nearly a century ago, from the beautiful valley of Snuff Mills and Oldbury Court and the countryside to the north of the city.

But why was the Frome nicknamed the Danny? None of the usually helpful local history researchers in Bristol have come up with any suggestions, either, and the 'Bristol Times' huge and knowledgeable readership has been unusually silent, too. There have been a couple of entertaining guesses. One is that it might have been inspired by the worldwide popularity of Johann Strauss' world-famous *Blue Danube Waltz* in Victorian times. Some joker quipped about the Frome being east Bristol's equivalent of the Danube, and this was shortened in Bristolian fashion to Danny.

Another is that the name comes from the Australian word 'dunny' (an outside toilet) which seems unlikely, until you read Latimer's Annals for 1850:

'The course of the Froom through the city was simply a sewer into which scores of smaller sewers poured their contents' he wrote. 'As a large section of the stream was uncovered, the stench which spread from it every summer often sufficed to turn weak stomachs'.

Even so, what would Aussie slang be doing in the middle of old Bristol? If this is the answer, did the nickname come from the many Australian troops at the huge military hospitals in Bristol during the First World War? The latest (and most intriguing) suggestion comes from C.W. Massey of Brislington, and I'd be interested to know if anyone else knows this story.

'I was born in Great Ann Street, back in 1928. My dad had a pony and trap and would take my mother and elder brother and sister to my gran's in Cannon Street. My grandfather told me that the Danny got its name from a young kiddie who was fishing for tiddlers and newts under the bridge at the end of Newfoundland Road, and somehow or other got drowned. They found his body under the steel bridge at the bottom of Peel Street and his mother was often seen on the bridge singing *Danny Boy* – perhaps his name? My grandfather told me this and I see no reason for him to lie to me'.

A fascinating tale and quite feasible, but is it really the origin of the name? Surely someone whose family has called the river the Danny for generations must know why.

Parks

Bristol has England's oldest public park – and a general reluctance to build any more.

Bristol seems to have the oldest public park in England, according to parks and gardens expert David Lambert. But the city has more than made up for this inspiring start by failing to provide any more parks unless pushed – and then failing to maintain the ones it had.

'Bristol is fortunate now in having a good proportion of public green space although this was not always so' said Mr Lambert in a new survey of the city's public spaces.

'In the nineteenth century when the city was less prosperous that in its earlier hey-day, the Corporation was generally reluctant to provide public parks. In the latter part of the twentieth century, the city council has been enlightened enough to buy for public use what were once great private estates: Ashton Court, Oldbury Court, Blaise, Kingsweston. Unfortunately the need for maintenance in

these larger areas has tended to divert attention and resources from the smaller public parks within the city. These neighbourhood parks are well loved by local people and tourists and they make a valuable contribution to Bristol's heritage'.

It's distinctly possible that Brandon Hill is the oldest public open space in the country – it was given to the city in 1174 by the Earl of Gloucester. But as the city grew, the main open space was the Marsh – now Queen Square – where until 1699 the public could enjoy bowls, bear baiting and fireworks. When the Marsh was taken over by developers, College Green became the main public area.

The history of College Green is one of continual redevelopment and neglect. In the seventeenth century it was ploughed up by sledges carrying clothes to dry on Brandon Hill and by huge and rowdy games of stop-ball. It was levelled and planted in 1703 and again neglected until 1756 when the great High Cross in the Centre was given to Stourhead because it got in the way of promenaders.

New squares with open spaces followed in the eighteenth and nineteenth century although most had access restricted to neighbouring households. But the most important public park was the zoo where as much emphasis was made of the landscaping and planting as of the animals.

New neighbourhoods grew up to support the city's industrial expansion but, as David Lambert pointed out, Bristol didn't build the kind of public parks found in the industrial towns of the Midlands and the north. While other councils saw parks as a vital leisure amenity for factory workers (and a way of keeping the workforce healthier and more productive), Bristol's few parks were only provided after pressure from workers' organizations and local do-gooders concerned about the dreadful health record of the city.

Tower of strength. The landmark Cabot Tower, on Bristol's popular Brandon Hill, was built over a hundred years ago to commemorate Cabot's voyage from Bristol to Newfoundland.

In 1847, Bristol's public parks consisted of Queen Square (6.75 acres), College Green (4.5 acres), Brunswick Square (1.25 acres), Portland Square (1.25 acres), and Brandon Hill (19.5 acres). Bristol was the third-most unhealthy city in England – yet nothing was done about providing more parks for another 40 years. With one major exception, that is. In 1861, the Corporation secured the Downs as a public open space for evermore (or at least until the zoo needed a new car park). The 'Bristol Times' claimed 'The Downs are now the People's Park', which was a bit silly considering it was in the middle of Bristol's wealthiest area and that residents had to be assured the common public would find it too much trouble to get there. But there was increasing pressure on the council to provide parks where they were really needed – in the working class areas of the city.

The council could have had land at Stapleton offered by Sir John Greville Smyth but didn't like the asking price or the fact that Sir John wanted it dedicated as a protected park, like the Downs. Councillors were shamed into looking at the problem again after several redundant churchyards were turned into public gardens, but rejected land off Newfoundland Road as too costly. That eventually became St Agnes Park.

It did open St Matthias Park (surrounded by a tannery, irons works and malt house), and accepted Sir John Greville Smyth's offer of 21.5 acres at Bedminster (now Greville Smyth Park, with a picturesque flyover running through it). And over the next 10 to 15 years most of Bristol's parks were reluctantly laid out and equipped, although the council turned down a chance to buy Arno's Vale estate and failed to provide a great central park like Bath's Royal Victoria Park. It took the Second World War and the destruction of the central shopping area before Bristol got that.

Since then every historic bandstand has been demolished, most drinking fountains

Downs fun: Generations of kids have amused themselves for free on this rock slide next to the Clifton Suspension Bridge.

have vanished and the Crimean War cannons and Victorian railing in several parks have been scrapped. Little parks have suffered as the council struggles to maintain the great estates, but there are signs that the situation is improving. At least these days park keepers are allowed one afternoon off a week and don't have to replace dead trees and shrubs from their own wages, as happened 100 years ago. And in 1998/99 alone, there were 16 million visits to Bristol parks, and the public voted them the second most important council service.

2 People

The Bristol girl who became the first woman doctor

Elizabeth Blackwell is a classic heroine of the feminist movement – the Bristol girl who fought prejudice and hostility to become the world's first qualified woman doctor.

She was born in Counterslip in 1821, the daughter of a sugar refiner and anti-slavery campaigner who had advanced beliefs about educating girls.

The family moved to Wilson Street, off Portland Square, and then to Nelson Street. But in 1832, the family refinery was destroyed by fire and it was decided to emigrate to America. The Blackwells subsequently became a focus for the anti-slavery movement, giving refuge to escaped slaves and campaigning for the boycott of sugar cane picked by slaves in favour of sugar beet. But Elizabeth's father died suddenly, leaving the family penniless. So the Blackwell girls opened a boarding school in their home.

By the time she was 24, Elizabeth knew French and German, studied philosophy and was a talented musician. But the rigours suffered by a friend dying from cancer persuaded her that she would like to be a doctor. She was warned of insurmountable obstacles and deep-rooted prejudice. But by teaching in the days and evenings as well as studying with a friendly doctor, she managed to make enough money to finance a medical course. She applied to 22 colleges and was rejected. She was advised to go to Paris or attend lectures disguised as a man. She refused, insisting that she must be regarded as equal to male students. Eventually, she was offered a place by a New York college, largely because everyone assumed it was a joke. Not surprisingly, being the only woman among 150 young men was not easy. But she was gradually accepted and when she passed her course with top honours, she became world famous.

Although she was a qualified doctor, she had problems in practising. She was refused admission to an obstetrics course so took midwifery. It was then she lost an eye to infection, ending her hopes of becoming the first woman surgeon. Her younger sister Emily would later win that honour. Elizabeth was offered a year on the wards at St Bartholomew's hospital in London but the ward specialising in women's diseases refused to let her in. She returned to America to set up a clinic for the poor and, in 1857, an infirmary for women and children staffed entirely by women. Among them was her surgeon sister, Emily. In 1859, she was registered as a doctor in England. Nine years later, her US hospital was recognised as a medical school and Elizabeth returned to Britain for good. Later, she became Professor of Gynaecology at the London School of Medicine for Women.

Early medic. Elizabeth Blackwell, who, against all the odds, managed to become the first qualified woman doctor in the world.

Pioneeer feminist. A fine oil painting by Joseph Stanley Kozlowski showing Bristolian Elizabeth Blackwell in her old age.

John Latimer, chronicler of Bristol

John Latimer was a Tynesider, yet he gave Bristolians a better understanding of their city's past than anyone who was ever born here.

The *Evening Post* diary column is named after him and it's doubtful whether any popular local history book could have been written without his astonishing research.

Latimer was born in 1824 and worked as a journalist in Newcastle, where he also produced a history book on the area. He then moved to Bristol in 1858, as editor of the *Bristol Mercury*, a position he held for 25 years. But his real life work was the production of his famous *Annals*.

The *Annals* were published in three volumes, covering the day-by-day history of Bristol from the seventeenth century onwards. For some reason, the nineteenth-century volume was published in the 1880s, which meant a fourth volume was required to take the story up to 1900.

The great pleasure of Latimer's *Annals* is the untypical mixture of dry council records, tedious debates and the usual Victorian

Annals. Journalist and editor John Latimer, the Northerner who saved Bristol historians years of work by producing his four volume Annals.

respect for the wealthy with a sardonic sense of humour and a dash of venom, a combination which betrays the author's newspaper origins. His verdicts on pompous councillors, brutal magistrates and hypocritical MPs are a joy, as are his hatchet jobs on Isambard Kingdom Brunel and the dreadful way the City Corporation treated the inventor of tarmac. However, wading through Latimer can be a chore, thanks to a very quirky index system, which turns inquiries into a game of guesswork. His habit of recording everything chronologically can also be intensely irritating – to follow a long story like the setting up of the Great Western Railway or the history of the docks means

referring to dozens of separate pages, reams apart from one another. But these are minor quibbles compared to the amazing depth of detail, the quirky sidelights, the anecdotes and the sheer wealth of information to be found in Latimer.

The real problem though is finding a copy. The Victorian originals fetch antique prices, and even the 1970 reprint is rapidly heading toward the £100 mark, if you can even find one.

It is really very sad, for if any book on Bristol deserved to be kept in print permanently it is Latimer's, a truly wonderful book that is as rewarding to read for sheer pleasure as it is for research.

John Gully, the bare-fist gentleman

If you know anything about boxing, you'll know of John Gully, the Wick innkeeper's son who battered Sixteen String Jack into submission and became a wealthy racehorse breeder and MP.

John lived in the days when boxing wasn't a namby-pamby sport with padded gloves and rules. Men faced up to each other with bare fists and bashed each other until one was too badly injured to stand.

Remarkably, these generally illegal displays of thuggery were regarded as a true science and the wealthy (known as 'The Fancy') bet fortunes on their favourites.

There was fierce rivalry between the champions of Bristol and Bath, and at a fair in Bath, huge crowds turned up to see Bristol's Sixteen String Jack face Bath's Flying Tinman. Jack was an 18-stone giant and the Tinman a mere 12 stone. After 20 minutes, Bath's champion was a bleeding wreck. The Bristol man was carried round the ring in triumph and boasted that if any more 'Bath squirts' needed polishing off, he'd take on a dozen and send them home in a cart to their mothers. No Bath men dared take him on, but John Gully from Wick did, despite the scorn of Jack, who said: 'Get the cart ready for in ten minutes I will send this babby home to his mother a-crying'. It didn't work out quite like that. After those ten minutes Gully had so trounced the Bristol giant that he couldn't stand, and had to be carted home.

Gully had learned his skill in boxing booths at the notorious St James Fair in Bristol. But he ended up in debtors' prison after a business he inherited foundered. He was rescued by The Game Chicken (Henry Pearce) an old Bristol friend who had become champion of England, and who persuaded The Fancy that Gully was worth a chance. They paid his debts, but demanded Gully fight the Chicken. After some decent food and training, Gully and the Chicken met in 1805. The fight lasted 75 minutes over 64 bloody rounds and, although the Chicken won, Gully so impressed the Fancy that he was given the backing he needed.

He moved to London where he beat man-mountain Bob Gregson twice. He seems to have been one of the few uncorrupted men in a dangerous world and the sporting aristocracy flocked to back him.

Soon he was able to give up the brutal world of boxing and move into horse racing. He became a respected member of Tattersall's, the famous London horse market; he bought and bred racehorses and was noted for running them honestly.

He became very rich and was elected MP for Pomfret. And, as the *Globe* newspaper recorded: 'He lived to a good old age and died sincerely regretted by all classes, from the prince to the peasant'.

Who could want a better obituary!

Bareknuckle fight. Henry Pearce, also known as 'The Game Chicken', gets to grips with prize-fighter John Gully during their famed encounter in 1805.

Ice cream family melts away

Very quietly and with no fuss, one of Bristol's best-known family companies has simply melted away.

The Verrecchias have been selling quality ice creams in the city for more than 70 years and introduced the first mobile ice-cream makers. They also took on national giants Walls and Lyons Maid in a battle against their monopolies on sales in small shops. Verrecchia was known to generations of Bristolians as Vereesha, regardless of the fact that the Italian pronunciation is 'Vereckia'. The family just sighed, accepted the inevitable and carried on selling some of the best ice cream in Bristol from their little Brislington factory.

Eugenio Verrecchia set up business in Bristol in 1925 after emigrating from Italy to Britain around the turn of the century. He opened the city's first ice-cream parlour, the Modern Café in Coronation Road, Bedminster, where Italian-style ice cream was made in huge wooden vats. These days, it's a Bristol & West branch.

In later years, company secretary Betty Verrecchia tried in vain to explain what made their product so special.
'It's traditional home-made stuff,' she said. 'We Italians started it all. But trying to explain the difference between Italian and English ice cream is like trying to say what's different about English and Italian pizza. If you go to Italy, you'll soon find out.'

Eugenio started it all, but it was Romeo and Maria who made the Verrecchia name a by-word for delicious ice cream in Bristol. Romeo was one of Eugenio's seven children, and he married Maria – known as Mrs V. to thousands of customers – in 1946. Romeo's brother Robert started the factory in Stockwood Road, Brislington, but it was Mrs V. who built up the fleet of vans which toured the city seven days a week. The family also ran three cafés in the city.

It was in 1960 that Verrecchia launched Bristol's first 'ice-cream machine on wheels', as it was then called. It was a real novelty. A wide-eyed *Evening Post* report stated:

'It means, in effect, that ice cream is made only minutes before it is served, unlike the days, and perhaps weeks, which the family brick type of ice remains in the refrigerator.

'An additional motor is fitted to the van to supply the generating power which works the machine and runs the freezing apparatus.

'Each morning the vans will leave with a complete load of mixed ingredients and will not have to return to the depot for refills. Cones are filled with ice cream by a tap similar to a miniature bar pump'.

The launch of the mobile ice-cream maker also marked the end of the Verrecchia link with Bedminster and the move to Brislington. By then the business had grown from one van to 36. Mrs V. died in 1991, aged 71, and Romeo died in 1993, aged 78. But the family link was maintained by Robert, his wife Betty, their sons Martin and Joseph and daughter Gian.

The hot summer of 1975 did wonders for the business, with production up by 50 per cent on the previous year, and a record output of 120 gallons of soft ice cream (7,200 cornets) and 18,000 ice lollies a day.

It was the same picture in 1990 when the staff worked a 14-hour day and Verrecchia sold nearly four million ice lollies and 100,000 litres of ice cream. And all the time the emphasis was on traditional quality. 'People want ice cream as it used to be,' declared Betty Verrecchia.

'They are fed up with newfangled things. We see it as a craft. With big firms, it's all economics. They start with the idea that they have so much to spend on packaging and so much for marketing. We have always done it

Champions. Betty, Gianna and Robert Verrecchia scooped first prize to win the Champion of Champions award for their coffee-flavoured ice cream.

the other way round and made ice cream according to the same recipe for 60 years. That's what's most popular.'

Betty and her sister Gloria had a starring role in the Oscar-winning film *The English Patient* as an accordion and piano duet. It was hardly a surprising choice – Betty was West of England accordion champion in 1950 and the film's director, Anthony Minghella, is her nephew and Gloria's son.

Now Verrecchia is no more. The van fleet and the remaining stock have been sold and the Brislington factory shut. The family has declined to say why.

Perhaps the reason lies in what Betty, now in her seventies, said back in 1990: 'None of us could bear to see the factory merged or taken over. It's been in the family so long. I suppose it's a bit of excessive pride.'

Film star. Betty Verrecchia, chairman of the ice cream company, took on another role when she travelled to Tuscany to be an extra in the Oscar winning film The English Patient.

The Bristol conman who built Australia

Highly expensive new flats have been built on the site of the old Limekiln Dock – that's the area opposite the SS Great Britain, formerly used for a timber yard and as part of the old gas works.

It was to No. 7 Limekiln Lane that Francis Greenway, Olive Greenway and John Tripp Greenway – how they were related isn't clear – moved from the isolate rural village of Mangotsfield to set up business as stonemasons, architects and builders.

Francis was probably the architect of the business and in 1806, a year after the company was set up, the Greenways were offered a design and build contract for a hotel and assembly rooms at the head of The Mall in Clifton. This was the time that Clifton was full of unfinished houses, which had been started speculatively with money made by slave, rum and tobacco trading. But war with the French led to a drying up of funds and many of the grand terraces remained half completed. The Greenways thought they could make a killing and bought a number of houses, which they completed and sold. They obviously overstretched themselves for in May 1809, they were declared bankrupt.

Old court records include among their assets 'marble in blocks, handsome modern chimney-pieces, Painswick stone slabs, pennant and other paving stones, figures in plaster of Paris after the antique, some finished to represent bronze, and two ornamental Gothic chimney tunnels intended for Portumnia Castle'.

It was around this time that Francis Greenway ran into a problem which changed his life and altered Australia for the better. He had a contract to finish a house in Cornwallis Crescent for 1,300 guineas. But after he was made bankrupt, Greenway alleged the owner had promised to pay an extra £250, but that he had lost the document. It mysteriously reappeared containing an endorsement from a lawyer backing Greenway's claim. Unfortunately the lawyer denied ever signing it, and Greenway was arrested. He admitted forgery at Bristol Assize and was sentenced to death, later commuted to transportation for life.

His supporters claim he was merely thinking of his creditors and that there had been verbal agreement about the extra payment. In any event, he was sent to Australia in 1813 where he became known as the father of Australian architecture. He designed a number of Georgian-style squares in Sydney and many public buildings and even ended up on an Australian banknote.

Olive and John Greenway seem to have got round their financial problems for they stayed in Limekiln Lane until around 1820.

When chemists doubled-up as vets

Butler's, the famous Old Market chemist, was just the prescription to cheer up patients who remember what was quite an extraordinary business.

But it seems that Tom Ward, who ran the place for most of this century, was not just a pharmacist who made up his own medicines on the spot. He was also a vet, a dentist and a moneylender. And if you needed insecticide, polish, ink, cough medicine for cattle, homemade wine, chutney or hair curling powder, Tom had a recipe for it. Remarkably, many of his creations have survived in a small mock leather book, dating back to Victorian times, which has been handed down to his family. It currently belongs to his grandson, John Jarritt and his wife Mary, who also knew the old man.

'He was a very gentle man, and very smart,' said John. 'He always wore a waistcoat with watch and chain and an ornate fob, and a trilby hat when he was out. We were on holiday with him in Exmouth when war broke out.'

Mary recalled: 'On Sunday evenings when my parents went to church I used to sit on his knee and comb his hair. It was quite luxurious.'

Tom Ward lived in Tyne Road, Bishopston, and was apprenticed in 1879 under stringent terms, which made him promise not to gamble, not to frequent taverns, not to go to playhouses – and not to get married. It's difficult to see what he did with his spare time.

The Jarritt's don't recall whether he started Butler's or took over an existing business. But when he died in the late '40s a lot of the original shop fittings went to the city museum. One of his most popular recipes was actually a bit of a cheat and would have Trading Standards storm troopers parachuting into Old Market these days. Brown eggs were more in demand that white ones on the spurious grounds that they were tastier. So, Tom offered a formula for turning white eggs into brown ones, which apparently sold rather well. Here is a selection of his other recipes. Don't try these at home – some of these materials are now regarded as dangerous in unskilled hands and recommended dosages of others have been changed.

Toothache Drops
Blend of oil of cloves, cannabis and chloroform. An alternative uses morphine, cocaine and alcohol which would certainly have deadened an aching tooth and probably everything else as well.

Shampoos
Mix sesqui-carbonate of soda, borax, soap and oil of verbena, or borax, spirit of camphor, and oil of rosemary.

Diuretic
Digitalis leaves, squill (a kind of lily), juniper berries, sherry and rectified spirit. Bruise solids, and macerate for five minutes in the solvent and then press and dissolve in the liquor. Add acetate of potassium and filter.

Sticky Fly Paper
One mustard tin of oil from a chip shop deep fryer after fish has been fried in it, mixed with a quarter of a coffee tin of resin.

Mahogany Polish
Mix shellac, benzoin, (aromatic gum from a Javanese tree), sandarach (powdered resin from a Moroccan tree) and methylated spirit.

Dr Bodie's Linament for Paralysis
Blend camphorate oil, turpentine, oil of thyme and chloroform in liquid ammonia.

Stove Polishing Paste
Blend graphite, sugar and oil of turpentine.

Ink
Tom had numerous recipes for different kinds of ink, including one mixed from tartaric acid, archil (red or violet dye made from lichens), nucilage (a kind of sticky gum), bicarbonate of soda, and nitrate of silver.

Tomato Sauce
Ripe tomatoes, chilli vinegar, garlic, shallots, salt, cayenne pepper and lemon juice.

Salad Cream
Salt, white sugar, best olive oil and two eggs added to cayenne pepper, mustard and malt vinegar.

Blackberry Wine
Blackberries, sugar, lemons, raisins, brandy and boiling water.

Old Market gem. This wonderful bow-fronted shop still exists in Old Market, but is unfortunately no longer a chemist.

There are plenty of other fascinating recipes for massage paste, piles cream, snuff, eau de Cologne, pick-me-ups, hair restorers, children's tonics, shaving cream, Indian brandy, jelly, spices and cleaners. But Tom's writing, never easy to read, has faded over the years (perhaps that's because he used one of his own inks) and many entries are in chemist's shorthand. But he also collected clippings from newspapers and magazines and stuck them in his book. Among them are the following tips:

• To make ginger wine, take 12oz of bruised ginger, 28lbs of sugar, 15 gallons of water, 2lbs of raisins, six Seville oranges and three lemons. Boil it all up, add cream, tartar and yeast, and mature it for six weeks.

• To brighten up the colours of caged birds, add iron sulphide to their diets.

• To preserve eggs, immerse in water glass (isinglass) solution.

• To make manure for pot plants, try half a peck (a quarter of a bushel which was eight dry gallons) of soot in 12 gallons of water with 1lb of guano (bird droppings) added.

• To treat chilblains mix carbolic acid, camphor copaiba (another tree resin) and chloroform, and apply to the affected parts with a feather.

The man who invented Wurzels

He plucked the Roses of Picardy, serenaded Danny Boy, stormed the walls of the Holy City and created the image of the Zummerset zider yokel.

His name was Fred Weatherly, he was one of the most prolific and popular songwriters ever – and he was born in Portishead 153 years ago.

Weatherly was a barrister who knew both Dickens and Gladstone and who managed to write 1,500 songs, many of which remain classics. He was the son of a country doctor, whose patients included survivors from the Battle of Trafalgar. As a boy he watched a funeral ship bearing he body of Lord Raglan, Commander-in-Chief in the Crimean War, passing up the Channel to Bristol and burial at Badminton. His mother came from Clifton Wood, Bristol, and was a gifted musician and singer who loved ballads and storytelling. Fred went to Hereford Cathedral School and wrote his first song at the age of 17. But it was a trip to see the Great Exhibition when he was just three that inspired one of his most famous songs, *Up From Somerset*, with its rousing chorus: 'Oh we'm come up from Zummerset, where the cider apples grow.' It did more than anything to give West Country folk a lasting Wurzel image.

He became a private tutor after university and his pupils included the King of Siam. He was actually invited to Siam to become tutor to the Crown Prince which, as has been pointed out on many occasions, might have led to the Rogers and Hammerstein musical *The King and I* being called 'The King and Fred' instead! But his songs were becoming well known – in fact Beatrix Potter's first published book illustrations were for Weatherly's *A Happy Pair*. A frustrated love affair in Portishead inspired songs like *The Girl I Love in Somerset* and *The Valley by the Sea*, while the pier master at Portishead was serenaded in *Captain Dando*.

His first wife was Anna Maria (Minnie) Hardwick, daughter of Worle surgeon John Hardwick, and they had one son and two daughters. Minnie died in 1920 and Fred married Miriam Bryan in 1923, at the age of seventy.

At the age of 39 he decided to change the course of his life and became a barrister and a pupil of Charles Dickens's son. He collaborated with the Italian composer Paolo Tosti on a series of romantic ballads and the pair serenaded Queen Victoria at her Diamond Jubilee party. He also translated Italian operas into English for Covent Garden. But it was what he called his Songs of the People that gained him the nickname of The People's Laureate.

He returned to Bristol in 1893 and lived in Whiteladies Road before moving to Edward Street, Bath, in 1910 for its more convenient rail connection. It was during these years that some of his most enduring songs were written. In 1902, he turned out *God Speed* for the opening of Avonmouth Docks and, in 1914, he teamed up with Ivor Novello to write a stirring recruitment number called *Bravo Bristol*. Other more durable songs from this period included *Danny Boy*, for which he wrote words to an Irish tune, which had allegedly been written by the Sidhe (Irish fairies). And there was *Roses of Picardy*, which touched the hearts of wartime listeners, and *The Holy City*, with its rousing chorus 'Jerusalem, Jerusalem, lift up your gates and sing.'

In 1923, he wrote his first opera and decided that the gramophone and wireless would never catch on. It was one of his rare mistakes. Two years later, he was elected a life member of Bristol Savages, a club for artists, musicians and writers, and his portrait still hangs in the Wigwam, their Park Row HQ. He performed in Portishead on occasions and the town library still has programmes for a 1926 concert of 'Songs Old and New' and a 1928 'Songs and Reminiscences' evening.

Fred died in Bath in 1919 and two years later Dame Clara Butt unveiled a memorial to him in the city. Proceeds from a Weatherly memorial concert endowed a bed in the Bath Royal Mineral Water Hospital. It is estimated Fred wrote 3,000 lyrics of which 1,500 were published. 'These songs are popular because people love to sing them' he once said. 'The heart of the people is still simple and healthy and sound.' Here's one of his classic songs that helped persuade local boys to go and fight the fiendish Hun.

Bravo Bristol

When the stalwart merchant venturers
Set out in days of old
They sailed with a Bristol blessing
To find a land of gold
And now there's a grimmer journey
There's a sterner call today
But the men of Bristol answer
In the good old Bristol way
(chorus)
It's a rough, rough road we're going
It's a tough, tough job to do
But sure as the wind is blowing
We mean to see it through
Who cares how the guns may thunder
Who recks of the sword and flame
We fight for the sake of England
And the honour of Bristol's name
And when the seas are free again
And the bloody fields are won
We'll tell our Bristol children
What Bristol men have done
Their names shall ring for ever
From Avon to the sea
And the sound of the march of the Bristol men
And the song of their sons shall be
(chorus)
by Fred Weatherly and Ivor Novello

Harriet Walter

Mrs Walter of Clifton offered a discreet service to Victorian parents – she disciplined their children to avoid them having to do it.

Campaigners who have succeeded in having the beating of children outlawed in Britain would have loved Mrs Walter. She offered a very special service to sensitive parents who felt their girls needed a good thrashing but didn't like to do it themselves – a Victorian 'Dial-a-Birch' in fact.

Mrs Walter operated at 53 Oakfield Road, Clifton, and advertised her respectable chastising service for unruly daughters in the national papers. One advertisement read: 'Bad temper, hysteria, idleness etc. cured by strict disciple and careful training'. Another claimed: 'Intractable Girls trained and educated. Excellent references. 'Hints on Management', 'Training of Children' and 'The Rod' 1s each. Advice by letter, 5s. Mrs Walter, Clifton'.

This was a bizarre enough idea, even by Victorian standards, for a bit of investigative reporting, and a magazine called *Truth* sent along some undercover agents. One of them, a woman, explained she had an unruly daughter she wanted 'broken in'. Mrs Walter offered to take the mythical unruly daughter for £100 a year and presented impressive references from the Dean of Lincoln, an admiral, a general, and a number of lords and ladies. Her guiding rule, she claimed was 'Never birch when angry'. She also revealed that she offered a travelling chastisement service as far away as London. If she was called up specially, she charged two and a half guineas: if she was already in London, the fee was 10s 6d.

The *Truth* team described her as a tall, strong woman, dressed like a nurse and wearing a Good Shepherd medallion, who was quite happy to describe her methods to

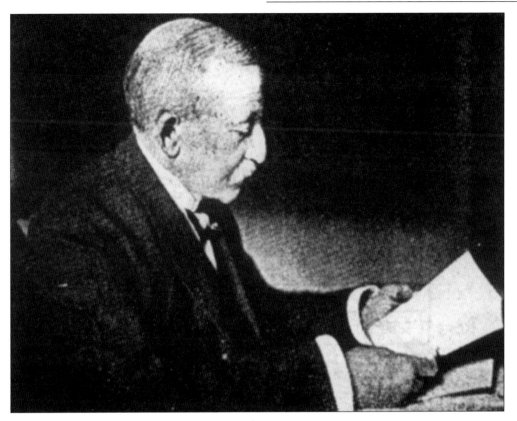

Danny boy. Portishead-born composer Fred Weatherly, who wrote 1,500 songs, including the famed Danny Boy, *in his lifetime.*

curious parents. She had a strong narrow table, straps for waist, wrists and ankle and a long pliable birch rod. The hapless victim had to take off her dress, knickers and corset and put on a dressing gown back to front – a bit like those embarrassing hospital gowns – and was quickly strapped down.

'Taking the birch, I measure my distance and, standing at the side, I proceed to strike slowly but firmly' Mrs Walter explained. 'By moving gently forward, each stroke is differently placed and six strokes may well be enough if given with full force. If the fault has been such as to need severe correction, then I begin on the other side and work back again. For screams, increased strokes must be given. If a girl tries very hard to bear it

bravely, then perhaps I give 10 instead of 12'. Remember that this was not a flagellation brothel but a respectable establishment in a high-class residential district and widely advertised, recommended and used. Even so, 'Mrs Walter' was not quite what she seemed. *Truth* discovered she was really Mrs Walter Smith, widow of the clergyman headmaster of All Saints School, Clifton, and she was so busy that she charged half a guinea just for an interview.

When her husband died, she set up a girls' school of her own and it was for this that the dean and the other VIPs had given references. No one had told them that Mrs Smith had quietly changed its purpose to a house of chastisement for difficult girls and

Georgian gem. Victorian Clifton, a haven of gentility and good taste in an increasingly industrialised city.

they were aghast when *Truth* published its finding. Mrs Smith suddenly found her establishment had lost all its big name supporters. The controversy over her activities filled the Bristol and Clifton newspapers' letters columns for some weeks and Mrs Clapp, Mrs Smith's birch supplier in St John's Road ('from a family who have made them for generations') panicked and denied ever selling them. It didn't help her cause that she had been advertising them for sale in the *Church Times*, of all places, six months earlier.

What happened to Mrs Smith? Did she carry on with her useful service for sensitive parents, or did she retire? Whatever happened to her, her story survives in numerous books as an example of the hypocritical and cruel underside of Victorian society.

Tom Cribb

Bare-knuckle fighter Tom Cribb, The Black Diamond, is a Bristol legend. And like all legends, he has attracted his fair share of myths.

Tom Cribb of Bristol, The Black Diamond, was undefeated Boxing Champion of England, yet there is no memorial to him in the city – not even Cribb's Causeway! In the eighteenth and early nineteenth century, Bristol was a major centre of prize fighting – that curious sport in which men toed a line and hammered each other into bloody oblivion. Someone once called the city 'the parsley-bed of pugilism'. In that case, Thomas Cribb was the sauce.

Thomas was baptised in the parish of St Philip and St Jacob on July 2, 1781, the fourth of ten children born to Thomas and Hannah (née Rogers) from St George. His grandfather, Isaac, also lived in St George and was described as a horse-driver. One of Thomas's younger brothers, George, followed

him into the ring, but had a short and unsuccessful career.

In 1794, at the age of 13, Cribb went to London and was initially apprenticed to a bell-hanger. It's probable that his parents wanted to get him away from one of the roughest areas of Bristol, for six Cribbs were either hanged or transported between 1800 and 1819. He became a coal porter at Wapping, a job which later gave him his boxing nickname of The Black Diamond. It was there he suffered two serious accidents (crushed between two barges and beneath a 500lb box of oranges) but recovered with no lasting ill effects. He then enlisted in the Navy before trying his luck as a prizefighter in January 1805. He rapidly defeated George Maddox, amazingly still fighting at the age of 50, and three other contenders, but went down to Bristolian George Nichols – the only defeat in his entire professional career.

In 1807, he was taken on by Captain Robert Barclay, a famous athlete, who offered to train and manage him and made him into the most celebrated pugilist of the day. His first match was against another great Bristol fighter, the one eyed Jem Belcher whose reputation was so high that the odds were six to four against Cribb. In fact Cribb beat him in just 35 minutes.

Cribb went on to beat two more opponents and when British champion John Gulley (another Bristolian) retired in 1808, Cribb was given the title.

Belcher was outraged and challenged him to a rematch in 1809 but was again soundly defeated. No one was prepared to take him on after that except a black American called Thomas Molyneux. The fact that Molyneux was both coloured and foreign aroused interest even among people who normally ignored boxing and Cribb was portrayed as fighting for the honour of England and the English. It was one of the hardest fights in Cribb's career but he finally beat Molyneux in 1810 and again at a rematch the following year when Molyneux collapsed after 19 minutes. The rematch demonstrated that Cribb had become a superstar in the days when fortunes depended on the verdict.

A crowd of 20,000 travelled the 100 miles from London to see the fight, including most of The Fancy – the upper class boxing fans headed by the Marquis of Queensbury.

The day after his victory, Cribb returned to London in a coach pulled by four horses decorated with blue ribbons and received a hero's welcome. He was later presented with a valuable silver cup. In 1812 at the age of 31, he announced his retirement and became a coal merchant. In six years, he fought 10 times and was only beaten once. For the next 15 years he sponsored and trained young fighters, including many Bristolians, acted as a second

Bristol's champion. Tom Cribb, Bristol's most famous pugilist, still has no memorial to his name in the city.

and gave exhibitions at sporting dinners. His coal business failed and he became a publican, but in 1814, after Napoleon had been defeated, he was chosen to demonstrate the skills of the pugilist before the Emperor of Russia, the King of Prussia, three Prussian princes, the Prince of Mecklenburg and Waterloo co-victor Marshall Blucher.

In 1819 he took over the Union Arms in Panton Street, just off the Haymarket, which was later renamed the Tom Cribb in his honour. In January 1822, he was offered the title of 'Champion for Life' although he gave it up the following year to his protégé, Thomas Spring. In 1821, he joined other boxers dressed in heraldic tabards as a guard of honour at the coronation of George IV. Some said they were there to protect the unpopular Queen Caroline from the mob. He might have been a great boxer but he was inept with money and a soft touch for a handout. In 1839, he was declared bankrupt and retired to Woolwich to live with his son. His last public appearance was in December 1822, when he was seen at a benefit fight for William Perry, the Tipton Slasher.

Thomas died on May 11, 1848, aged 67 years, and was buried in the churchyard of St Mary's and St Andrew's, Woolwich. The cause of death was said to be a stomach disease and exhaustion. A subscription fund was opened for a memoriam and, in 1854, a Portland stone lion with its paw resting on the champion's belt was erected in the churchyard. The inscription read: 'Respect the ashes of the brave'.

Over the years many legends have grown up about Cribb, who rarely returned to Bristol in his days as a boxing star. Among them were claims that he owned a greengrocer's shop in Passage Street, and that he trained at the Hatchet Inn, the Rummer, the Greyhound, or the Black Horse, Easter Compton. He didn't – neither did he work coal barges at Hanham or retire to Conham

Vale. And Cribb's Causeway has nothing to do with him at all – it was named that long before Thomas was born.

That's a pity because there's nothing in Bristol to commemorate one of the city's greatest sporting stars, and one who is largely forgotten.

William Worcestre

William Worcestre was the man who measured medieval Bristol by the length of his own 'steppys' – the distance from heel to toe of his pointy shoes. His remarkable record of the old city has now been published in modern English for the first time.

Despite his name, William Worcestre was born in Bristol in 1415 and became secretary and agent to Sir John Fastolf, the knight often credited as the inspiration for Shakespeare's rumbustious Falstaff. Between 1477 and 1480, he travelled widely and recorded what he saw in incredible detail, leaving an unrivalled record of much of medieval England.

In 1478, he surveyed St Mary Redcliffe church, then without a spire after it had been demolished in a storm. Two years later he was back and in a month meticulously measured and recorded buildings and streets, from great churches to public latrines.

He was staying with his recently widowed sister, Joan Jay, the wife of merchant venturer John Jay, and wandered the city, measuring and chatting to locals like stonemasons, the porter at Bristol castle, a local hermit and a young blacksmith rock climbing in Avon Gorge. He wandered as far as the chapel of St Anne at Brislington, and heard about a

Hidden vaults. One of the underground cellars in Bristol's High Street. It's now closed to the public because of continual problems with flooding and access.

65

hawthorn tree that used to stand in the centre of town before the High Cross was put up in 1373.

Every Bristol historian has quoted William, but his notes were in Latin and his handwriting was pretty awful. Now his unique survey of Bristol in 1480 has been published by Bristol Record Society with both the Latin text and a modern English translation. Worcestre's 'steppys', or steps, incidentally have been worked out at measuring 21-22 inches (56cms).

To give you a flavour of this quite remarkable book, here is William Worcestre on:

Hill Fort on Clifton Down

The hill fort upon the high ground not quarter of a mile from Ghyston Cliff (Avon Gorge) was founded there before the time of William the Conqueror by the Saracens or Jews, by a certain Ghyst, a giant portrayed on the ground. And because so great a hill fort was probably built in ancient times, it remains to this day as a circle of great stones lying thus, in an orderly ring and great circle whereby a very strong castle is seen to have been there which hundreds of years ago has been destroyed and thrown to the ground.

The Hot Well and Cave

There is a spring about a bow shot (distant) at the Black Rock in the depth of the river on the Ghyston Cliff side and its is as warm as milk or the water at Bath. Foxhole (now named Ghyston's Cave) is a remarkable cave situated high up on Ghyston Cliff, upon a ledge of the highest rock and it is an exceedingly dangerous spot for getting into the cave lest one fall to the depths of the water 60 fathoms and more below.

The Castle

The tower called keep is 25 feet thick at the base and nine and a half feet at the eaves under the lead roofing and 60 feet in length east to west and 45 feet north to south with four towers standing at the four corners.

Washerwomen

Worcestre discovered two stairways (or slips), each of 80 stairs, rising from The Back to near Baldwin Street and the Chapel of St John the Evangelist where women did their washing. 'Sometimes I have seen 12 women at a time washing woollen cloths and other household items. For the goodwives when the tide there flows back towards the sea, so that the River Avon coming from Bristol Bridge shall be clear and fresh, so then they do their washing.'

Ships

Ships, boats and skiffs, also boats called woodbushes, ketches and picards, are from the ports of Welsh towns (which Worcestre names). They moor their ships at The Back on the rising tide to unload and discharge the ships of their goods.

St Anne's chapel, Brislington

The square candle, the gift of the Weavers' Guild, measures 80 feet in length, width eight inches, thickness seven inches. Each square candle, in weight of wax and manufacture, costs £5.

The Crypt on Bristol Bridge

Upon Bristol Bridge there is a beautiful large crypt, skilfully worked, below the chapel of the Blessed Mary, for accommodating the councillor and officers of the town of Bristol and for meetings on the public business of the town.

The Shambles

The extremely high and spacious halls of the King with vaults in the street of Worship Street, otherwise the Shambles or Butchery... there are three extremely deep cellars of the King beneath three halls of great size and built high, which were established for the safekeeping of wool and merchandise for

Old Bristol bridge. Shops, houses and a church lined old Bristol bridge, a medieval gem swept away by increased traffic and highway improvements. It also blocked the river at this point, and no ships could move upstream.

loading Bristol ships for foreign parts beyond the seas.

Cellars

Worcestre identifies 163 cellars and vaults in High Street, Broad Street, Corn Street, Pithay, Wynch (Wine) Street, The Shambles, St Nicholas Street, Small Street, Horse Street and Broadmead, with many more in Redcliffe Street.

Hannah More

Hannah More was either a notable religious and social reformer or a right wing bigot who did her best to keep the rich man in his castle and the poor man at his gate.

Hannah More is one of those people who sound fascinating at a distance, but who must have been utterly intolerable in real life. She was an unmitigated snob, never happier than when in the company of the rich and famous; a religious bigot, a campaigner against women's rights and Catholics, and founder of schools for the poor which taught them to be good and pious servants – but not how to write.

She was a friend of royalty, yet was so badly bullied by her domestic staff she had to move house. And while one minister called her 'one of the most truly evangelical divines of this whole age', essayist Augustine Birrell said 'She flounders like a huge conger eel in an ocean of dingy morality' and buried her 19 books in his garden in disgust at 'one of the most detestable writers that ever held a pen'.

She was born in Frenchay, fourth of five daughters of a Stapleton village school-master, in 1745. She learned several languages, improving her French by chatting to French prisoners-of-war on parole, before becoming a teacher at her sister's school on College Green, Bristol. While in her teens she came under the influence of Anglican cleric Dr James Stonhouse, who she called her conscience. Her first book, *Select Moral Tales*, was printed in Gloucester by Robert Raikes, founder of the Sunday school movement. An Edward Turner of Belmont, Wraxall, courted her, proposed and was accepted but (perhaps understandably) backed out on no less than three occasions. Dr Stonhouse intervened and Turner agreed to pay Hannah an annuity in recompense for her injured feelings. He also left her £1,000 in his will.

Hannah was certainly a woman of contrasts who wrote a number of successful plays, before deciding that the theatre was immoral. In 1732, she visited London for the first time and met such luminaries as writer Alexander Pope, actor David Garrick and painter Sir Joshua Reynolds. Reynolds in turn introduced her to Dr Samuel Johnson, who was highly irritated by her excessive flattery of him but who did help her with her poetry.

One of her plays, a turgid tragedy called *Percy*, was a great success and a translation was found among Mozart's effects when he died. It is thought he may have been considering using it as the basis of an opera. By this time, however, Hannah had turned against the theatre as something unchristian and wouldn't attend. She also rejected what she had once called 'such agreeable and laudable customs as getting tipsy twice a day on Herefordshire cider'. She turned more and more to fundamentalist religion and even railed against saying 'Merry Christmas', on

the grounds that the word 'Merry' suggested 'idle mirth and injurious excess'. But although she was now writing only religious dramas, she still turned out secular poetry and Dr Johnson called her 'the finest versifatrix in the English language'.

Her hatred of non-Christians grew – when she heard of the death of the 'malignant' Gibbon, author of the classic *Decline and Fall of the Roman Empire*, she commented 'How many souls has his writing polluted?' But she was a strong and effective campaigner for the abolition of slavery, and helped Ann Yearsley, the Bristol milkmaid poet, to improve her grammar and poems.

Hannah and her sisters moved to Great Pulteney Street in Bath and then to Barley Wood, Wrington, where they entertained royalty and basked in their approval. It was then Hannah set up the chain of village schools for which she is best remembered, starting in Cheddar with backing from anti-slavery campaigner William Wilberforce, and then Rowberrow, Shipham, Sandford, Draycot, Banwell, Congresbury, Yatton, Axbridge and Nailsea. But her pupils were taught 'such coarse work as may fit them for servants' plus her unyielding brand of Christianity, and she 'allowed no writing for the poor'. The schools faced opposition from farmers who feared the effects of religion on their workers and, six months after her death, all had closed.

She was enthusiastic about the French Revolution at first but soon turned against it, accusing the revolutionaries of anarchy and, even worse, atheism. She was equally incensed by Tom Paine's influential *The Rights of Man*, which argued in favour of republicanism, declaiming: 'From liberty, equality, and the rights of man, the Good Lord deliver us.' She also refused to read Mary Woolstencroft's unrelated *Rights of Women* on the grounds that women were not fit for government, 'To be unstable and capricious is but too characteristic of our sex' she said.

Instead she bombarded the poor with religious tracts and recipes for scrag ends of meat and vegetables, and wrote a book called *Village Politics* which urged the labouring classes to reject all thoughts of bettering their God-given situation in life. In a century where the middle classes enthusiastically sang: 'The rich man at his castle, the poor man at his gate, God keep them high and lowly, and each to his estate', her homilies sold in their millions. They attracted enthusiastic praise from churchmen but virulent criticism from outside, which she shrugged off. She was, she believed, invariably right and opponents of her views were condemned as anti-Christian and destined for Hell.

Her religious novel, *Coelebs in Search of a Wife*, was a best-seller, as were her strongly anti-feminist books on bringing up daughters. She castigated ordinary novels as showing 'vice with a smiling face' and became almost an icon to evangelical Christians. As she grew older, and even more bigoted and intolerant, she put the French on her ever-growing list of hates, warning that peace with France after Waterloo was a worse evil than war. She was still a dreadful snob, delighting in praise from the aristocracy, opposing any attempts to give Catholics the vote and refusing membership of the Royal Society of Literature because she felt 'her sex alone a disqualification'.

By this time, Holy Hannah, as she was known, was almost an invalid and confined to bed for months at a time, and her family and friends were diminishing. She was spending money faster than it was coming in and her servants at Barley Wood were running riot, stealing and partying and neglecting their work. In the end friends stepped in, sacked the servants and sold the house. Hannah was moved to Windsor Terrace, Clifton, where she died in 1833 at the age of 89.

Holy Hannah. She was a blue stocking who championed the anti-slavery cause but not the rights of women or the poor.

M.J. Crossley Evans, who wrote a life of Hannah, believes she was a woman who 'upheld practical Christianity and did incalculable good in inculcating Scriptural values at all levels of society. She was the enemy of vanity, debauchery, atheism and Sabbath breaking, a tireless worker for King and country, an upholder of the established order and an enemy to the philosophy and literature of the Enlightenment.'

He might have added that she was also affected, an arrogant elitist, and a strong campaigner against improving the lot of the poor, women or Catholics. Throughout her self-righteous life, she did as much harm as she did good. She is remembered these days in Hannah More Primary school, St Phillips, and in Hannah More Infants, Nailsea. What is more surprising is that her reputation remains intact and has never suffered from the kind of reappraisal of Bristol's heroes that turned Edward Colston from noble benefactor into evil slave trader.

Final resting place. Despite dying in Clifton, Hannah More was taken back to Wrington to be buried with her sisters. The family home, Barley Wood, was situated just outside the village.

Fishponds birthplace. Hannah's father, Jacob, was a schoolmaster here when she was born in 1745. The building is still standing.

Martin Frobisher

A new theory about Martin Frobisher, the man who brought Eskimos and worthless rock to Bristol.

A great Elizabethan hero, who brought the first Eskimos ever seen to Bristol, has been dubbed a conman who even tried to cheat Queen Elizabeth herself.

Sir Martin Frobisher was one of the many adventurers who tried to find the fabled north-west passage to Cathay (China or Japan) across the top of Canada. It has long been known that he brought back some ores from what he claimed was Cathay and that they were stored in Bristol Castle until they were found to be worthless. Now Canadian archaeologist Dr Reginald Auger claims that not only did Frobisher deliberately try to pass off worthless rocks as valuable but that he abandoned part of his crew to avoid them spilling the beans.

Frobisher first sailed to arctic Canada in 1576 and brought back rocks containing what assayers showed contained silver and gold. One theory is that he used silver-contaminated lead in the refining process. He returned the following year and brought back a staggering 200 tons of rocks, which he found on what is now Kodlunarn (White Man's) Island, and for a third time in 1578 when he returned with 12 shiploads of ore. It was on the second voyage in 1577 that he sailed into Bristol after meeting with a Bristol ship plundered by the French and in dire straits. Here, he unloaded his cargo into the castle where it was tested, but the assayers could find no trace of any precious metal. It was also on this trip that Frobisher brought back three Eskimos who rapidly died from pneumonia. But one of them first delighted Bristolians by hunting ducks from a kayak in the harbour.

What Dr Auger and his team have now found on Kodlunarn Island is the remains of a laboratory where Frobisher may have tested the rocks before bringing them back. And this, says Dr Auger, suggests Frobisher knew all along that the rocks were worthless, but was trying to defraud his financial backers, including the Queen. 'We cannot prove it' he said in *British Archaeology* magazine, 'but the idea is perhaps supported by the mysterious disappearance at sea of the 1578 expedition's laboratory records'.

A judge was appointed to investigate the whole affair and demanded that Frobisher's chemists hand over the records of their experiments on the island. Sadly, it seems, they were lost through a porthole left open during a storm on the way back.

Even more intriguing is Dr Auger's theory about the fate of Frobisher's crew. Inuit (the proper name for Eskimos, which is actually an insulting description) tradition has it that tribes-people helped a group of abandoned Europeans survive the bitter Arctic winter before they built a ship to escape and presumably died at sea. The archaeologists have now found that stores stockpiled on Kodlunarn had been raided and timbers taken – apparently to build a boat. Were those left behind mutineers – or were they honest men who threatened to unmask Frobisher's attempted fraud when they got back?

Whatever the truth, and whatever explanation Frobisher gave for shipping tons of useless rock to Bristol and London, it did him no harm. He went on to sail to the West Indies with Francis Drake in 1585 and was knighted for his role in the defeat of the Spanish Armada in 1588 when he commanded a ship called the *Triumph*. He died in 1594 from wounds received at the siege of Crozon in France.

Castle grim. A sketch of old Bristol castle, as Martin Frobisher would have seen it when he sailed into Bristol.

Beverley Nichols

Who today remembers Beverley Nichols, best-selling author of sickly sentimental prose from a gentler era?

Nichols was born in Bower Ashton, Bristol, on September 9, 1898. Beverley's parents, John Nichols and Pauline Shalders had three boys, Paul, Alan and then John Beverley, who, as he grew up, was determined to be famous in some way. He was educated at Marlborough and Balliol, wrote his first novel, *Prelude*, when he was 22, and by the late '20s was rubbing shoulders with the rich and famous of the day.

One diary entry from the time – and one that was far from unusual – reads:

'Breakfast with Lloyd George
Lunch with Diaghalev
Tea with Sean O'Casey
Cocktails with George Gershwin
Dinner at the Garrick Club with H.G. Wells.'

He was a fine pianist but adored flowers since making his first daisy chain as a little boy. In *Garden Open Today* (1963), he thought what fun it would be if he could pay for gardeners who couldn't afford to go abroad to see the wild mauve irises around Nazareth, the bougainvillea on the walls of Tangiers, the golden ferns of Trinidad, the golden mimosa in Australia, and the white orchids in the mountains of Darjeeling.

Minor events like the First World War failed to dampen his enthusiasm – he was wounded and being carried by stretcher along the North-West Frontier when he spotted his first wild striped pink and white tulips, like the ones in old Dutch flower paintings. In Corfu, he found cascades of Sternbergia daffodils; in Portugal he was delighted to find hoop-petticoat daffodils, just six inches tall with flowers no bigger than a thimble.

Down The Garden Path was dedicated to 'Marie Rose Antoinette Catherine de Robert d'Aqueria de Rochegude d'Erlanger, whose charms are as gay and numerous as her names'. He was invited to stay with her in Venice, but she mixed up the dates. He found his room covered in thousands of pieces of glittering multi-coloured glass from Venetian chandeliers, waiting to be put together! Later, she invited herself to stay with Beverley at his Down-The-Garden-Path cottage at Glatton, which rather alarmed him as there was only well water, one small bathroom and no room for a maid. But although she could be as grand as the Queen of Sheba, she fell for its charms and adapted immediately.

His garden at Glatton was full of flowers in summer, and with snowdrops in February. He would gather a big bunch and arrange them in a bowl on a circle of mirror, so that he could see not only reflections inside the flowers, but twice as many as he'd picked. He also loved cats, and had six, called One, Two, Three, Four, Five and Seven. He missed out Six, as it wouldn't have been quite nice to call 'Sick! Sick! Sick!' at the end of the day!

'Although he was a complicated man, it doesn't show in his garden books' said one Nichols fan, 'You have to read his autobiographies, *The Unforgiving Minute* and *Father Figure*, which is quite outrageous, to find the real man. Even then you're not quite sure'.

Some idea of the precious Nichols style comes in *Garden Open Today* where he describes the Green Dragon Lily as 'a regal lily powdered with the dust of emeralds, flowering by moonlight in a green glade'. He was also noted for playing Chopin to a white vase full of freshly picked apple blossom. The blossom seemed to enjoy the recital – 'The sunlight danced over the keys, the apple-blossom swayed, ever so slightly' he wrote.

He kept cheap reproductions of French Impressionists like Renoir, Turillo, Degas, Monet, Manet, Cezanne and Matisse inside the lid of his desk as his own little art gallery.

When he died, his ashes were scattered at his beloved Glatton, followed by a memorial service at St Paul's, Covent Garden, two months later on November 16 – the 50th anniversary of the publication of *Down The Garden Path*. Derek Jacobi, Michael Hordern, Patrick Ryecart, Mervyn Stockwood and Liz Robertson were there remembering him that day, and Frances Day and John Mills sang 'Little White Room' from Floodlight, a 1938 revue set to Beverley's music and lyrics.

Country cottage. Beverley Nichols life was dominated by flowers. His garden at Glatton was a riot of colour.

George White

George White was a remarkable and energetic businessman who changed the way Britons travelled from birth to the grave.

If George White had had his way, you might be catching a train from Bristol to London from a stylish station on The Centre. George was a director of the Bristol and London and South Western Junction Railway, which had ambitious plans to compete with the Great Western Railway. And he campaigned for a big station where the War Memorial now stands, which would have meant trains being sent across Somerset to join the existing line into Waterloo. If it had ever happened, it would have dramatically changed the development of the city and made a proper bus-train interchange possible. But the rival Great Western Railway was too powerful and its influence ensured that the idea never got off the ground. It was one of the few setbacks in the career of one of the most remarkable men in Bristol's history. George White achieved far more in the city than Brunel or anyone else, come to that, yet even today his name is nowhere near as famous as Brunel's.

'The greatest man among us,' said one obituary. 'His name will live forever', said another.

George White's legacy to the city includes the biggest aircraft centre in Europe, the main hospital, the public transport system, and some of its finest buildings. He was the inspiration behind the massive expansion of Bristol's tram (and later bus) system, which eventually covered a huge area of western England. He also ran so many other tram systems around the country it could be said he virtually invented commuting.

He came up with a successful scheme to link Canon's Marsh with Avonmouth docks and the Midland railway network, via the disused Port and Pier Line along Avon Gorge. He made a spectacular financial killing by outwitting Stock Exchange speculators when George's Brewery shares were put on sale, and another by buying and selling the Severn and Wye and Severn Bridge railway.

He launched the first electric tram service in Britain (from Kingswood to St George), made an unsuccessful bid to run underground trains in London, and received his knighthood through the recommendation of the Prime Minister.

He was also a great benefactor. He set up a remarkable free pension scheme for tramways workers, wiped out crippling debts holding up the building of what is now Bristol Royal Infirmary, founded the Bristol branch of the Red Cross, and backed garden suburb housing to replace slums.

It was also Sir George who recognised the future of public transport was in motor buses, rather than trams. He launched Bristol's first bus service and motor taxis, and expanded into car and lorry hire, hearses, charabancs, Clifton Rocks Railway, and a South Wales coal mine. Despite all this, Sir George is probably best remembered for his most far-sighted decision – to invest in the new science of flying machines. In 1910, he had set up four companies, including Bristol Aeroplane Company. His first, disastrous venture was licensing a dubious French design which turned out to be too heavy to take off.

His famous Bristol Boxkite did better, and demonstration flights on the Downs were watched by thousands. Bristol planes sold all over the world, won competitions and set new standards. Filton was actually planned as one of a national chain of air stations – forerunners of airports. He set up flying schools across Europe, and 308 of the 664 pilots in the First World War came from his schools. He even backed an extraordinary underwater aircraft which could be towed by ships to destroy submarines and mines. Known as a paravane, it saved thousands of lives.

Sir George died in 1916 shortly after a speech in which he suggested workers should take shares in their employers' businesses 'to secure the heart and soul of every man working in the shop.'

'I could sweep the world if I had a few thousand men who were imbued with feelings of that kind, who had the same interest as I had myself in that business,' he said.

James Nayler

James Nayler paid a terrible price for his delusions of divinity.

He was Bristol's Mad Messiah, who rode at the head of a procession of chanting followers into Bristol through Bedminster on an October day in 1656.

Nayler, an itinerant preacher in the south-west, was convinced that he was the re-incarnation of Christ. And several of his followers, particularly the women, were inclined to believe him. So when he rode from Somerset into Bristol on a donkey, imitating Christ on his journey to Jerusalem, his path was strewn with garments and tokens of thanksgiving, and the streets resounded to shouts of 'Hosannah!'

He left Bedminster heading a procession of his followers, and rode into Bristol 'amid screams of rejoicing' and was promptly arrested by the magistrates. He was examined in the Tolzey court, where he repeatedly proclaimed he was the Messiah and the perplexed magistrates handed the case over to Parliament.

Nayler and some of his followers were taken by horse to London (at a cost of £37) and a long inquiry was started by a Commons committee. They found the charges of blasphemy proved, and took 13 days to decide on the punishment. It was vicious: On December 17, the Commons decided that Nayler should be exposed in the pillory for two hours at Westminster, then whipped to London for another two hours in the stocks. Then he was to have his tongue bored through with a red-hot iron and his forehead branded with the letter B, and sent back to Bristol where he was to ride through the streets on a bare-backed horse and be publicly whipped. As if this was not enough, the unfortunate Nayler was then carried back to London to solitary confinement, without pen or paper, and forced to earn his food by hard labour until Parliament thought fit to release him.

Public opinion was shocked at the proposed punishment, and after Nayler had been brought to the verge of death by 310 lashes, Governor Scrope of Bristol brought a petition for mercy. It was ignored. Nayler had his tongue and brow branded and the crowd, far from reviling him, began to see him as a Christ-like martyr.

He was brought back to Bristol on January 17 to Newgate Jail, tied on horseback facing the horse's tail, and paraded through the city

Mad Messiah. Deluded James Nayler, convinced that he was a re-incarnation of Christ, rode into Bristol on a donkey.

where he was stripped, tied to a cart horse and whipped from one end of Bristol Bridge to the other.

After his wounds healed in prison, he was sent back to jail in London, and eventually released. He returned to Bristol in his old age 'apparently delivered from his mental distemper.' But for some years, he was still defended as 'the Quakers' Jesus.'

Mikael Pedersen

Mikael Pedersen was a Dane who invented a curious bike, among other things, and is buried in Gloucestershire.

Danish-born genius Mikael Pedersen is buried today in Dursley, the Gloucestershire town where he built an astonishing bicycle more than a century ago.

Yet his final journey was even more bizarre than his extraordinary life. Pedersen was buried in Copenhagen in 1929 after he died in poverty in an old people's home. But although he was largely forgotten in his own country, Pedersen cycle fans in Britain wanted their hero remembered. So, in 1995, Pedersen's remains were dug up and shipped to Dursley in a vintage port wine box.

'One must not be flippant about such things, but he liked a drink, and I think he must be laughing at that,' said the Revd Patrick Birt, a Dorset minister and Veteran Cyclist Club member. 'There is a Pedersen cult. It is something that grabs you! It is an amazingly comfortable bicycle.'

Mikael Pedersen was born on October 25 1855, the eldest of seven children. He became a fine musician, but was apprenticed to an agricultural equipment factory.

His first invention was a self-clearing threshing machine which he hired out to local farmers, but his wealth was made from developing a centrifugal cream separator.

Meanwhile in Dursley in 1867 Robert Ashton Lister was setting up a small iron foundry and farm equipment factory. Pedersen liked what he saw and became one of the first shareholders of R.A. Lister & Co. – later the world-famous diesel engine manufacturer Lister-Petter.

Pedersen loved cycling but felt he could do better than the ungainly Victorian penny-farthing and the smaller so-called safety machines. So he designed the bike which has become an icon among cycling historians. It was distinctive – some say eccentric – with its unique cantilever frame and hammock-style saddle, and was first made in 1897 in Dursley.

At first it was built mainly from wood but Pedersen later turned to metal tubing. The Dursley-Pedersen works employed up to 50 people and turned out 20 to 30 cycles a week. The machine was light, comfortable and stylish, but never cheap, and his customers tended to be wealthy – the Sultan of Morocco, the Marquis of Anglesey, and army top brass among them.

Pedersen soon became a familiar figure in Dursley with his black bushy beard and Norfolk suit, but his life did not run quite as smoothly as his bicycles. He divorced two wives because they could not bear him children, then produced three sons and a daughter with third wife Ingeborg who he married in 1906.

Yet, like many brilliant inventors, he was no businessman. Business fell off and after an operation for cancer of an eyebrow, he seemed to lose interest in his invention. He returned to Denmark, leaving all his property and money to his second wife, Dagmar.

Yet the Pedersen cycle lives on with fans all over the world and it is still made in Burton-on-Trent, Germany and Denmark. But if you want one, it will set you back more than £1,000.

But why move his remains from his own country? Dursley town councillor and retired

Cycle inventor. Mikael Pederson was a brilliant inventor but not so good as a businessman.

Finally at rest. Pederson's remains were finally re-buried, with a new headstone, in a Dursley plot in 1995.

Methodist Minister the Revd Ernie Clarke said at the time that not everyone believed it was a good idea, but his relatives approved. 'Pedersen's remains would have disappeared completely if they had stayed in Denmark,' he said. 'This will be a little tourist attraction, for Dursley – Pedersen is part of the town's history.'

Bristol monumental masons, Mossfords, donated a black granite memorial, depicting the inventor on his bicycle, which now stands above the grave in Kingshill cemetery. And at the internment ceremony, which was attended by Pedersen fans and their bikes, a tape was played of one of Pedersen's own compositions. Who could ask for a better send-off?

Twos company. The low slung Pederson cycle gave a very comfortable ride, even for ladies in the long skirts of the time.

Reginald Dyer

Was a Long Ashton pensioner really a brutal mass murderer, or just a military man who made a mistake?

The argument still rages today – was Reginald Dyer a brilliant general who quelled a potential rebellion, or a callous killer who mowed down 379 innocent people?

Dyer, who spent his last years in Long Ashton, ordered his troops to fire without warning on a peaceful open-air meeting in Amritsar, holy city of the Sikhs in the Punjab. He insisted to his dying day that he was right, but an official inquiry called him inhuman and war minister Winston Churchill wanted him charged with murder. Now the debate over Dyer's role in the 1919 massacre has been reopened by the publication of the official papers on the incident which have been buried in the Stationery Office archives. They show Dyer as an arrogant, brutal bully, even by the standards of his time, and one with little respect for human life.

Amritsar was in uproar when Dyer arrived, after the British authorities had expelled two popular independence campaigners. European women and children were herded into the fort for safety as mobs rampaged through the streets in protest. Troops fired in self defence and a number of rioters were killed. The situation deteriorated, and banks, the railway and telegraph office were attacked and British staff brutally murdered. A missionary called Miss Sherwood was knocked off her bike and badly beaten up, and the mob tried to kill European hospital workers and destroy Christian buildings. Then Brigadier General Reginald Dyer arrived to take charge. He declared martial law and banned all mass gatherings but, as the Stationary Office papers reveal, there is no evidence that most of the inhabitants of Amritsar ever heard about the restrictions.

On April 13 1919, there was a gathering of between 10,000 and 20,000 people in an enclosed park not far from the famous Golden Temple. Many were peaceful villagers from surrounding areas. Dyer placed his troops on both sides and, without any warning, ordered them to fire. The troops shot 1,650 rounds over 10 minutes and left 379 dead and 1,200 wounded. Dyer freely admitted later he had aimed at where the crowds were thickest.

He also agreed he would have turned machine guns on his armoured cars on the crowd but they were too big to get into the park. 'I was going to punish them' he told an inquiry. 'My idea from the military point of view was to make a wide impression. I wanted to reduce their morale'.

Hero or murderer? Debate still rages over General Dyer's role in the deaths of 379 innocent Indian people.

But Dyer also conceded that he hadn't needed to shoot at all. 'I think it quite possible that I could have dispersed them without firing,' he agreed. 'Then they would all come back and laugh at me'.

As hundreds lay dead and dying, Dyer marched his troops away and made no attempt to help the wounded. 'It was not my job,' he said, 'The hospitals were open and the medical officers were there. The wounded had only to apply for help'.

The inquiry which followed concluded that the massacre had irreparably harmed British interests in India and was as horrific as some of the German Great War 'frightfulness' in Belgium and France. But Dyer hadn't finished.

In the street where Miss Sherwood was attacked he ordered all Indians to crawl on all fours, including innocent residents who had no other way of getting out of their homes. He also had six unconvicted prisoners flogged on the spot on the dubious grounds that they just might have been the attackers. 'The chances were that these were the particular men,' he insisted. 'These men had in a dastardly fashion beaten a woman and knocked her down six times in the street. Nothing was too bad for them'.

The inquiry verdict was unequivocal. 'We feel that General Dyer, by adopting an inhuman and un-British method of dealing with subjects of His Majesty the King-Emperor, has done great disservice to the interest of British rule in India,' it declared. 'This aspect it was not possible for people of the mentality of General Dyer to realise'.

But Dyer had powerful supporters who claim his actions had halted a full scale rebellion. He was simply sacked from the army under a cloud, and a few years later, a judge ruled he had acted correctly.

He retired to St Martin's Cottage, Long Ashton, in 1926, and died the following year. 'I only want to die and know from my Maker whether I did right or wrong' he said. After a service at the parish church, he was given a full military funeral at St Martin-in-the-Fields, London.

But his legacy of hatred lives on in Amritsar and in 1997 Sikhs tried to get the Queen to apologise for the massacre during a royal visit. They didn't get one: instead Prince Philip un-tactfully expressed doubts about the death toll mentioned on a memorial plaque, claiming: 'That's wrong. I was in the navy with Dyer's son'.

Vivian Stanshall

A new biography came out in 2001 of Vivian Stanshall, vocalist with the '60s group the Bonzo Dog Doo Dah Band, who lived in Bristol for a while. This is a personal memory by 'Bristol Times' editor David Harrison of the Thekla days.

I first got to know Vivian through his wife, the novelist Pamela Longfellow. She is an exotic, energy-charged and endlessly fascinating half Iroquois, who is now known as Ki, and who still talks to Vivian. It would be nice to think this book has his blessing.

Pam was one of two women who dreamt of running a showboat which would be a centre for arts and entertainment, food and drink, experiments and tomfoolery. But, unlike most dreamers, they did something about it. In fact they bought an old Baltic coaster called the *Thekla*, sailed it into the centre of Bristol's ancient harbour (which was then being transformed from working dock to leisure area) and bullied the planning department into letting them stay. The ship was renamed *The Old Profanity Show Boat*, a choice which did nothing to endear these buccaneers to the stiff-necked local councillors. And, thanks to a mixture of animal cunning, negotiating skills, sheer bluff and the odd bit of eyelash fluttering, the *Old Profanity* was

launched as Bristol's first floating theatre, music venue, bar and dream boat. It would need another book to really tell the whole, strange, bizarre story of the *Old Profanity* – Ki always insists these days that it worked for as long as it was relevant and needed and it died when its time had come (it is still there, horribly enlarged and extended, but little more than a standard city club these days).

At the time, Vivian and Pam (as she was) were living apart. Vivian's career was always on the point of taking off in a big way again, but the potential was too often drowned in alcohol and self pity. The Bonzo Dog band were a diminishing memory, Rawlinson's End appealed more to a cult audience. It seemed that the second greatest voice of the century as someone put it, was destined to end up as voice-overs for commercials. (The greatest, according to this same source, and since you were wondering, was allegedly Orson Wells. Some might argue for a reversal in that order).

But Vivian had a dream of his own and that was his own musical. Not a *Sound of Music* or even a *Tommy*, but a musical within the same anarchistic, surrealist, open-ended framework as the Bonzo's. Pam had a stage, and the slightly more down-to-earth approach needed for the mundane necessities like funding, costumes, sets and the like. The couple wrote the script, Vivian took care of the songs, the music, the arrangements and directing, and the newly-formed Crackpot Theatre Company (what a typically anachronistic name) was born. The show was called *Stinkfoot* and subtitled An English Comic Opera.

I still have the programme, and the characters listed sum up the Stanshall vision perfectly – The Left Half of Screwy the Ocean Liner's Brain, The Partly Cooked Shrimp, The Balanced Nose, Mrs Bag Bag – while the players and backstage workers were among the best Bristol could offer.

At home. Vivian Stanshall in the deck house of the Thekla *where he worked surrounded by plants and paraphernalia.*

I went to interview Vivian for the first time in the wheelhouse of the *Old Profanity* where he was working. He'd turned it into a kind of conservatory but a Vivian-style conservatory, complete with strange musical instruments, curious momentos, and sketches for the show on the bulk heads. I still have one of them on the wall, above where I write.

He was quieter, more hesitant, less ebullient than I expected. I didn't know then about his personal problems. But what really fascinated me was his magnificent mous-tache, a glorious sweeping cutlass-shaped appendage which looked as if it might eventually curve right back and take root in his temples. It was a Flying Officer Prune moustache, a cad's moustache, the sort of creation stroked sneeringly by villains in Victorian melodramas. It looked more at home in the nineteenth-

century hothouse he had created in the wheelhouse than Vivian did himself.

He talked quite seriously about *Stinkfoot*, about its genesis and imminent birth, about the promises of funding from showbiz chums to take it to London, a few words about his new life in Bristol. There was little, though, of the urban spaceman, of the man who could sing about Jollity Farm without seeming stupid, and who mercilessly send up the once vital questions of whether blue men could sing the whites or what colour to paint half a shared drainpipe.

He wasn't well. It showed and looking back at photographs of the time reinforces memories of a crippled giant, a mighty, creative ego in self-forged chains.

On one visit later, he asked if I would walk with him to Bristol's Theatre Royal, a few

Family: Vivian and Ki (right) with daughters and friends outside the Thekla *on a snowy winter day.*

hundred yards from the ship. But those few hundred yards were across Queen Square, the largest Georgian square in Western Europe. Vivian was seriously agoraphobic and there was an awful lot of sky to fall on him in Queen Square. We walked to the edge of the square where he took a deep breath, caught hold of my arm and, as I led him across, he stared at the ground, and talked constantly – rambled really – about anything to keep his mind off the zillions of tons of air pressing down on his head.

A really fit Vivian (and a less caring and loving Pam) might have seen the longueurs, the self indulgences, the unnecessary fat in *Stinkfoot*. On the first night, it went on endlessly, desperately in need of sharp scissors and a less involved director. Oh, it was a good show, full of vivid imagination and invention, some gorgeous songs and some quite superb singing. The sets and costumes were marvellously realised and the cast played their hearts out. There was just too much of it, that's all.

On that first night, I spotted Vivian sitting at a quiet table with Pam, crying. Why? I have never felt the need to ask. That's between them, and even noticing it accidentally seems an intrusion. After *Stinkfoot* moved to London, I never saw Vivian again. News of his death wasn't, somehow, unexpected although it seems a grim and sordid way to go for a man with his head in the clouds. If he'd had a chance, he'd have stage managed something really spectacular and memorable.

I remain close friends with Pamela/Ki via email, and still have that original Vivian sketch on my wall and some of the scenery for *Stinkfoot* in my attic. Even better, my little grand-daughter loves the music of the Bonzos, and 'Jollity Farm' and 'Mr Slater's Parrot' are again heard across the land, entertaining a new generation. When I wrote to Ki that Vivian would be delighted if he knew, she replied simply 'he does'.

Poseur. Two typical publicity pictures (above and below) of Vivian hamming it up for the camera.

3 Two Sides of Bristol

Ghost train to the skies

The airport of the stars is a booming leisure area now, and the Ghost Train has long been shunted into a siding. Whitchurch airport, once the most important in Britain, is a fading memory and the Ghost Train little more than legend.

And without people like Bristol ex-pilot and writer Ken Wakefield, the extraordinary history of the old Whitchurch airport would be lost for ever.

This was once the city's airport, a large open area in the shadow of Dundry Hill. It opened in February 1930 and the first plane to land was a de Havilland DH 60 Moth belonging to Bristol and Wessex Aeroplane Club. The 298-acre site had previously been part of Filwood and Tyning farms and Bristol Corporation paid 52 pounds an acre for it. If all had gone well, it would have been a major hub in the network of international airports slowly growing across Europe.

But the Second World War got in the way and the site was hemmed in by housing and hills. It couldn't expand to meet demand and in 1957 it closed. Bristol airport moved to the little airfield at Lulsgate – a sad error in retrospect, when Filton was better placed and ripe for development.

These days the only planes that use the old runway are model ones and the old airport has been renamed Hengrove Park. It's difficult to imagine now that this development area was once classed as Britain's most important air link with its friends and allies.

'It's a distinction earned during the darkest days of the Second World War, when its role as the country's main air gateway to the free world was a closely guarded secret,' says Ken Wakefield in *Somewhere in the West Country*, an amazingly detailed history of the airport's 27 years of life.

'At the time, news reports covering the arrival of Very Important Persons mentioned only an aerodrome *Somewhere in the West Country*, but many must have guessed this was in fact Bristol (Whitchurch) airport.'

After the expansion years of the 1930s, Whitchurch was well placed as a wartime airport. KLM Royal Dutch Airline planes which had escaped the Germans were based there on charter to British Overseas Airways. So was a Danish Airlines Focke Wulf, which was scheduled to fly the Royal Family to Canada if the Germans invaded. The most important route out of Whitchurch was to neutral Lisbon in Portugal, a dangerous run involving a wide sweep out into the Atlantic to avoid the Luftwaffe.

No RAF planes were ever based there but the airport played a vital role just the same. And that is where the Ghost Train came in.

Anonymous but instantly recognisable people came down from London on what was soon nicknamed the Ghost Train and gathered at the city's Grand Hotel until their flight was ready.

High flyers. Pleasure flights, like this one from Whitchurch airport, were very popular in the inter-war years.

It's doubtful whether the full list of VIPs will ever be known but those confirmed included Queen Wilhelmina of the Netherlands (flying in tennis shoes) and Prince Bernhard, the Crown Prince of Norway, Sir Samuel and Lady Hoare (and butler) and Mrs Eleanor Roosevelt, wife of the American President. There were plenty of film stars too, flying in to entertain US forces via Lisbon or Ireland. Among them were Bob Hope, paying a rare flying visit to his home town; Bing Crosby, Dinah Shore, Edward G. Robinson and Joe E. Brown.

It's rather ironic that most of the incidents at Whitchurch were either accidental or deliberate sabotage rather than enemy action. As Ken records, two Hurricanes crash-landed

after failing to find Filton in low cloud and rain, several other planes overshot the runway and a BOAC de Havilland crashed with a fuel line fault, hitting a cottage.

But two other de Havillands were deliberately destroyed, set on fire by a disgruntled BOAC employee. Nevertheless, by 1941, the fleet operating out of Whitchurch had risen to 50.

'BOAC was indispensable,' said Ken. 'Throughout the war it performed magnificently but at no time were its land plane and flying boat services more valuable than during the bleak 1940/41 period, with Whitchurch playing its part in full as one of Britain's few gateways to the free world. However, the role played at Whitchurch was never revealed in

Pioneers. Happy passengers on the first Aer Lingus flight into Whitchurch airport in 1936.

wartime. For security reasons, it was always referred to simply as a West Country airport'.

Every variety of land and seaplane used by the RAF and Fleet Air Arm passed through Whitchurch, including secret prototypes of advanced aircraft and even the RAF's first operational jet, the Gloster Meteor.

The Luftwaffe, by chance or design, generally left the Lisbon flight alone. It might have been because it was useful, of course.

Veteran journalist, the late Max Barnes, reckoned British agents were flown to Portugal from Whitchurch and German agents returned by the same route. It all seems rather gentlemanly now.

'The Luftwaffe turned a blind eye to the Lisbon service because it served the German purpose to do so,' claimed Barnes. 'So Whitchurch saw the strange spectacle of bundles of British newspapers fresh from the presses being loaded on to Lisbon-bound aircraft. On arrival the papers were eagerly snapped up by Axis agents.'

One Lisbon flight was attacked in November 1942 but managed to escape into cloud. Another in May, 1943 was less lucky – it bumped into a patrol of eight long range German fighters and was shot down. Among the 17 who died were two children and film heart-throb Leslie Howard.

One theory is that agents at Lisbon had reported a passenger they thought was Winston Churchill or they got Howard mixed up with R.J. Mitchell , designer of the Spitfire, who he was playing in a film. The

Airport aerial. A 1930s picture of Bristol's airport, which was then based at Whitchurch, on the city's outskirts.

German squadron leader, who was new to the sector, said simply they thought the plane was an RAF flight and they had not been told that civilian travellers were in the area.

Even so, in the three years to 1943, KLM flew 1,622 flights in and out of Whitchurch, carrying nearly 10,000 passengers. That's a success rate of 94 per cent, a figure some peacetime airlines would envy. The most unexpected landing at Whitchurch was probably a big USAF B24 Liberator loaded with bombs which the crew promptly dumped on the runway. It was too big to take off again so was dismantled and taken away on trucks.

One upside of the Lisbon trips was the raffia baskets of fruit which crews brought back and distributed to staff and children in hospital. The empty baskets were much sought after, too, in rationed Britain.

The unsung heroes of the Air Transport Auxiliary who flew planes of all sizes and shapes around the country to where they were needed were based at Whitchurch, too. During the war, the ATA ferried 308,567 aircraft of 147 different types and lost 154 flight staff.

After the war, the airport reverted to a civil airline terminal and was tipped as a major international hub. But the problems which the bigger wartime planes had in landing and taking off made it obvious it would never work and the inevitable happened.

These days, the airport is commemorated in Airport Road (part of the Bristol ring road) and in the Happy Landings pub. But you'll seek in vain for a memorial to the Ghost Train.

When the city council gunned-down ratepayers

When Bristol City Council starts charging citizens to drive into their own city centre, there may be the odd mild protest or two.

But it's doubtful whether the council will react quite so forcibly as their predecessors did the last time Bristolians protested against tolls.

On that occasion, they called in troops, shot a number of innocent ratepayers, then covered up the whole incident so no one was ever blamed. Perhaps we shouldn't be giving College Green ideas, but it's only 200 years since 14 people were gunned down on Bristol Bridge in one of the worst civilian massacres Britain has ever seen.

Michael Manson of Sefton Park Road, Bristol, spent seven years sifting through reports, hand bills, broadsheet ballads and other sources to try to get at the truth of what really happened.

'The Bristol Bridge massacre is a topic that has been ignored by Bristol's historians,' he said. 'Due to a cover-up by Bristol Corporation to avoid its incompetence being made public, little has been written about this tragic event until now.'

The new Bristol Bridge, which replaced a cramped thirteenth-century crossing with houses on it, was opened in 1768 with tolls charged to help pay for it. By 1793, the atmosphere in Bristol was highly charged, with war against the French hitting business badly and extreme nervousness spreading among the powerful sectors of society, about the Earth-shattering ideas behind the bloody French Revolution – that ordinary people had rights, too.

It was against this volatile background that Bristol Bridge tolls were put up for auction, despite the fact that the building costs had long been covered. Everyone expected the tolls to be dropped. Instead, thanks to bungling by the trustees, the reserves had dropped to below the level needed for maintenance, and it was decided to extend the lease. These were the days when Bristol Council elected itself and spent a small fortune every year on wining and dining members. They were responsible to no one and published no accounts, and the same people nominated each other for the exclusive club of councillors, Merchant venturers and magistrates. Democracy was a far-off dream; the minority held absolute power in the city and they were determined to keep it. Consequently it was the combination of a corrupt city establishment and the fear of revolution that brought the tolls controversy to a head.

The toll collector, Abraham Hiscoxe, realised that his job was likely to be increasingly unpopular and declined to renew his contract. He abandoned toll collection, and a carter forced his way across the bridge without paying. A crowd gathered, barrels of

Beautiful bridge. The elegant new Bristol Bridge of 1768, pictured here in 1824. It was controlled by tolls which were very unpopular.

beer were breached and the tollgates burned. The Corporation did nothing, but the bridge trustees offered a reward for capture of the arsonists and warned the death penalty still existed for taking down toll boards. The toll charge was reinstated.

Nine days later, new gates were put up and were promptly set on fire again. This time magistrate, councillor, former MP and bad-tempered bully George Daubeny was on the scene. He started cursing the crowd and lashing out at innocent bystanders, and was knocked to the ground. The mayor panicked and called troops from Stapleton where they were guarding French prisoners.

The Riot Act was read, warning people to disperse or face the death penalty. It simply inflamed the crowd and Daubeny ordered the soldiers to fire above the heads of the crowd. The mob fled but one man, labourer John Abbot, was hit by a stray musket ball. He later died.

The following day, during the annual mayor-making, Daubeny joined toll collectors to see the new charge was levied. Within minutes a crowd gathered and Daubeny again inflamed the situation by assaulting an innocent coachman who was caught up in the crowd. In the end, tolls were again suspended.

On Monday morning, traffic jammed the streets on both sides of the bridge. Tempers flared, the militia were called back and the Riot Act read three times. Daubeny once again stirred things up by attacking an innocent bystander and dragging him off to Newgate Prison by his feet.

The situation worsened, even though the soldiers were withdrawn, and the crowds grew alarmingly. Another set of tollgates were burned and the returning militia driven off with stones and mud. What happened next isn't clear. But the soldiers knelt and someone gave the order to fire. A volley was aimed straight down St Thomas Street and into the crowd. The back row of troops then turned and fired in other directions, leaving no avenue of escape. More than 100 rounds were fired.

By the time it was all over, 14 people were dead or dying, around 45 injured and a number facing amputations. Many were simply people passing by who had got caught up in the crowd.

Coroners at the following inquests refused to allow the jury to return a verdict of 'willful murder by the person or persons who ordered the militia to fire' because a magistrate or councillor might be blamed. They did allow the jury to blame the deaths on 'murder by person or persons unknown' which was bad enough.

The Corporation and town clerk Sam Worrall (better known for his involvement in the Princess Caraboo fraud) tried to dismiss the dead as 'indiscrete and blameable' for still being there after the Riot Act was read. This led to further disturbances and soldiers parading the streets of Bristol with drawn swords. But the whole incident was rapidly hushed up and (unless censored) the minutes of the council show it was not even discussed (the price of turbot was more interesting).

The bridge toll was never reinstated but councillors were plagued for years afterwards by broadsheets, ballads, savage satires and poems attacking their (and especially Daubeny's) roles in the massacre. An independent public inquiry fizzled out when it looked like the mayor and Daubeny might be named as the people who ordered the militia to fire, and the question of blame was quietly forgotten. It was as big a scandal as the massacre itself.

To find out more, try reading the excellent *Riot! The Bristol Bridge Massacre of 1793*, published by Michael Manson's Past and Present Press.

Boating weather. One of the most famous comic novels ever written, Jerome K. Jerome's Three Men in a Boat, *was published by Arrowsmiths.*

Timetables. Published in 1854, Evans and Arrowsmith's penny Time Table of Steam Packets and Railway Trains *was a surprising bestseller.*

Three men in a cellar

Two of the best-loved comic books of all time began life in a Bristol cellar.

Few people remember the Bristol link, but if it wasn't for the vision of a local publisher, neither book might have made it to the shops.

One was George and Weedon Grossmsith's classic tale of the suburban Pooter family, *Diary of a Nobody*. The other was an equally timeless story of a trio of friends meandering down the Thames, called *Three Men in a Boat*. And both were published as a bold act of faith by J.W. Arrowsmith, once better known as a publishers of railway and steam packet timetables.

Arrowsmith was based in Quay Street, off the city centre, and was anxious to break into general publishing. So Isaac Arrowsmith persuaded a friend to write what was then called a 'shilling shocker' which, to the author's bemusement (he was an estate agent called Fred Fargus) became a big seller.

It was titled *Called Back*, issued by Hugh Conway, and it put Arrowsmiths on the literary map. Within a few years, the firm was publishing leading writers such as Arthur Conan Doyle, Marie Corelli and Anthony Hope. Jerome K. Jerome, a young humorous writer who had already penned *Idle Thoughts Of An Idle Fellow*, had a new book he wanted to sell, and he approached Arrowsmiths after hearing good things about the company. Mr Arrowsmith read the manuscript and thought the book might 'do well in the summer months'. He wanted to publish it in his popular Shilling Library but Jerome insisted on 1s 6d because he wanted his book illustrated. In 1889, *Three Men in a Boat* appeared and was slaughtered by the critics. The public, however, loved it! The book was published all over the world and sold particularly well in the German and Russian translations. It made Jerome comfortable, but hardly rich, because many editions were simply pirated. In America, for instance, it sold more than a million copies, but Jerome didn't receive a cent.

Today, the book is as popular as ever and has sold well over three million copies in English alone.

An evocative account survives of the Arrowsmith's annual outing or waysgooze: 'Mr Arrowsmith led out the men in his employ to enjoy a rustic holiday' it reads. 'At 8am, they assembled around his breakfast table in Berkeley Place, which was bountifully covered.

'The great day ended when at 11 p.m., the omnibus was loaded with the company, 12 in number, and thence rolling on to Clifton, the night was rendered harmonious by the hearty songs of John Bull.'

Pay up for criticising the council

Householders criticising city council plans would have got short shrift in Cabot's day.

The council then knew exactly how to deal with rebellious citizens who wouldn't do what they were told by those who knew best.

Criticism bred unrest, thought councillors, so they tackled it firmly and resolutely. So, from 1422, anyone saying nasty things about the mayor, council or their officials was landed with a whopping fine. Those were the days!

A few years later in 1497, the law came in very handy after customs officer Thomas Norton accused Mayor William Spencer of treason in open court and actually threw down his gauntlet as a challenge. The mayor protested his innocence, but agreed to stand down and go to prison until King Edward IV

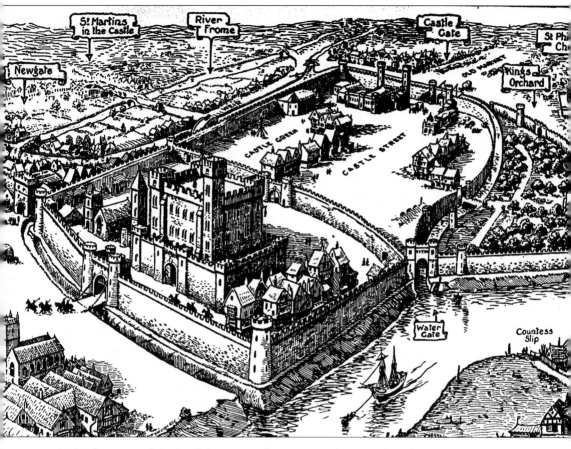

Mighty fortress. Bristol Castle, which was reputedly a s strong as the Tower of London, and whose scant remains can still be seen in Castle Park, played a major role in the early history, not just of the city, but of the whole kingdom.

could judge the case. Considering the state of prisons in those days, that was a very brave move.

Eventually Norton and the mayor appeared before the King, when a deputation from the council praised Spencer as a first-class chap and condemned Norton as a blaggard. He had robbed and threatened members of his own family, they claimed, and spent his nights in taverns, his mornings in bed – and even played tennis and other immoral sports instead of going to church. He also employed a gang of thugs, an offence for which the mayor had prosecuted him and the reason why, said councillors, that Norton

had laid the charges.

Norton fought back strongly, insisting his gang were merely assistants who helped him seek out contraband. He also alleged the mayor was himself a smuggler and that he had prosecuted Norton because the customs man had refused a bribe of a barrel of wine to allow through some untaxed cloth. But Norton was unable to back up his charge of treason with evidence and the case was thrown out. What became of him is unknown, but it probably wasn't pleasant.

In 1399, Bristol wisely backed Henry Bolinbroke when he deposed Richard II and turned himself into Henry IV.

When Henry arrived in Bristol, three of Richard's favourites – Scrope, Bushy and Green, described by Shakespeare as 'the caterpillars of the Commonwealth' – were holed up in the great castle. When they surrendered, they were promptly beheaded by the High Cross. Their heads were sent to London in a basket with a note from Henry, inquiring sweetly which side the Londoners were on.

A few months later, the Bristol mob set upon the Earl of Gloucester, another of Richard's supporters, and cut off his head, too, as a sign of loyalty. Henry, ever-generous, gave the earl's furred gown to the leader of the mob as a thank-you gift.

In the years leading to the Wars of the Roses, Bristol backed the Yorkist cause – not surprising, as the Duke of York owned land at Kings Barton and had powerful friends in the city. The Lancastrian Henry VI was not amused and Bristol was forced to buy a general pardon for its citizens. But, when Henry sent gunpowder to Bristol for safe keeping, the mayor seized it and used it to prepare Bristol Castle against a Lancastrian attack.

For once, the council backed the right horse and the Yorkist Edward IV was duly grateful, celebrating by beheading a few unrepentant Lancastrians by the High Cross. But Bristol rapidly changed loyalties and backed Henry VI again. The result was the kind of anarchy that led to the fight at Nibley Green, (near the modern M5 North) between Lord Berkeley and Viscount Lisle, the last battle between private armies fought on British soil.

This time Bristol got it wrong. Edward smashed the Lancastrians under Margaret of Anjou (who Bristol had welcomed and helped) at the Battle of Tewkesbury, and a number of prominent Bristolians were killed. Edward was more lenient than most medieval monarchs and gave a general pardon to the city, although eight leading citizens lost all their property.

By the time Giovanni Caboto (John Cabot) came to Bristol, Edward had been replaced by his brother (Richard III) and then by Henry Tudor (Henry VII). And it was this Henry who, 500 years ago, gave Cabot the licence to take a Bristol ship to seek out the sea route to Cathay.

Awkward birth of a towering vision

Bristol's most prominent landmark, the Cabot Tower, was 100 years old in 1998. But the official opening was marked by a disastrous fire, a confidence trick and some rather clever council penny pinching.

The foundation stone of the Cabot Tower was laid on Brandon Hill in 1897, the 400th anniversary of John Cabot's journey to the New World.

It was supposed to simply commemorate the Matthew's journey, until someone on the council came up with a great idea to help raise the cash. Money for the tower had to be found from public subscriptions, and the promoters encouraged wider interest with a neat bit of marketing. They pointed out that it was also Queen Victoria's Diamond Jubilee Year, so the tower could double up as a memorial to 'the 60th year of Her Majesty's glorious reign'. Clever stuff; it raised £5,000.

By July 1898, the 75ft tower (105ft to the top of the spire) had been completed at a cost of £3,250, but it was decided to defer the formal opening until September when the British Association was meeting in the city. All was ready for the biggest party of the year, when disaster struck.

The celebrations were due to be held in the Colston Hall, but on the night of September 1, the building was gutted by fire and the banquet was hurriedly moved to Bristol Grammar School's great hall. The

Going up! A rare picture of Brandon Hill's famous Cabot Tower under construction over a hundred years ago. It was built of red sandstone and Bath freestone and cost £3,300.

tower was officially opened by the Marquis of Dufferin and Ava, former governor-general of Canada, in the presence of Canadian and American representatives and most of the local bigwigs. A huge crowd turned out, although whether they would have heard the many speeches in the days before public address systems is doubtful. Then the VIPs headed off for their party, leaving the general populace to marvel at Bristol's latest wonder.

It was at the banquet that Lord Dufferin thanked God that Cabot had got to America first (which, of course, he didn't), thus ensuring that the continent became a bastion of the Anglo Saxon race instead of being occupied by 'an alien people' – i.e. the Spanish and Portuguese.

It was also there that Louis de Rougemont made a small piece of history. De Rougemont claimed to be a Frenchman who had just returned from living for 28 years among the aborigines of Australia. He gave a graphic account of his adventures to spellbound banquet-goers and even read a much-appreciated paper to the British Association meeting. Red faces all round, then, when it was discovered that his name wasn't de Rougemont at all and that he had made up the whole remarkable tale.

The tower itself was designed by W.V. Gough in what is called a Tudor Gothic style, and the spire is topped by a gilded figure representing commerce mounted on a globe. But it could have been a statue of John and Sebastian Cabot instead, and sited on the Downs.

There was quite a debate in the Bristol newspapers 100 years ago over the design of a monument to mark the 400th anniversary of Cabot's historic voyage from Bristol. One John Fisher came up with a plan for a statue of John Cabot, peering earnestly ahead at the coast of America with his teenage son Sebastian there at his side. Fisher went as far as modelling his idea in clay and suggested

that it should be placed by the Observatory on Clifton Down. Bristolians didn't like that, and Brandon Hill was finally settled on as the site.

Local artist Samuel Loxton – whose many black and white line drawings of the city are still much prized – came up with a very grandiose scheme. He envisaged a tower, 100ft high and rather like the one eventually built, but with big rooms inside to be used as a museum or picture gallery. It would be approached by a double flight of steps on either side of the base, which would be surrounded by a promenade area. The design finally chosen was much simpler, with just an internal staircase to the viewing platform at the top.

Bristol has a Cabot Tower to mark Cabot's departure from the city. Newfoundland also has one on Signal Hill, St John's, to celebrate his arrival there.

Its Cabot memorial was also built in 1897 to mark the 400th anniversary of the journey, but it looks more like a small fort and it contains a shop and information centre as well as a viewing platform.

The Great Fairs and the Corsairs

Bristol's Great Fairs are little more than a memory now, recalled only in street names like Horsefair and Haymarket.

But in their day, they were regarded as the most crime-ridden and dissolute markets in Britain.

And they were so famous that, for centuries, the Navy had to patrol the Bristol Channel at fair time to stop visitors being attacked or kidnapped by pirates and slavers.

The annual St James' Fair in September was such a magnet for traders that, in 1636,

All lit up. The Tudor Gothic style Cabot Tower, 105ft in height, specially lit up for the Festival of Britain in 1951.

12 Turkish warships were spotted off Cornwall, waiting to waylay people heading to Bristol. And every year there were reports of raiders hanging around the sea approaches to Bristol, looking for rich pickings in slaves or trade goods, and navy frigates patrolled regularly to frighten them off.

It may have been St James' Fair, the best known, which brought one of the many outbreaks of plague to Bristol in the seventeenth century. The City Corporation at the time was deeply concerned that the disease would travel to Bristol on goods brought in from London. It banned all leather goods and upholstery, but the London wholesalers appealed to the government, saying they made most of their annual income at Bristol. The government quashed the Bristol ban, and left the city open to infection.

But what a spectacle St James' Fair must have been, despite its reputation for wild characters, assault, robbery and all kinds of sex for sale.

Historian John Latimer left a wonderfully evocative description of the fair at its height.

'Blankets and woollens from Yorkshire, silks from Macclesfield, linens from Belfast and Lancashire, carpets from Kidderminster, cutlery from Sheffield, hardware from Walsall and Wolverhampton, china and earthenware from Staffordshire and other counties, cotton stockings from Tewkesbury, lace from Buckinghamshire and Devon, trinkets from Birmingham and London, ribbons from Coventry, buck and hog skins for breeches, hats and caps, millinery, haberdashery, female ornaments, sweetmeats and multitudinous toys from various quarters arrived in heavily-laden wagons and were joined by equally large contributions from the chief industries of the district.

'To these again were added nearly all the travelling exhibitions and entertainments then in the country – menageries, circuses, theatres, puppet shows, waxworks, flying coaches, rope-dancers, acrobats, conjurors, pig-faced ladies, living skeletons, and mummers of all sort who attracted patrons by making a perfect din.

'It need scarcely be added that the scene attracted a too plentiful supply of pickpockets, thieves, thimble-riggers and swindlers of every genus.'

The fair attracted everyone, from the Duke of Beaufort's children to the offspring of the rowdy and dangerous Kingswood colliers. There were stalls everywhere and what Latimer calls 'standing places', wooden constructions that took a month to build.

But as the years went by, the business side of the fair gradually decreased and the entertainment side increased, as did the number of bush houses (unlicensed drinking dens). The nine-day fair gradually extended to become a fortnight and, as Latimer puts it, 'a centre of corruption and demoralisation.'

Everyone piously condemned the fair, but made so much money out of it that nothing was done. In 1813, a St James church member even offered £3,000 – a huge amount then – to have the fair suppressed. It was contemptuously rejected as much less than the profits made.

St James was one of two great Bristol Fairs; the other was St Paul's, which took place on March 1 at the end of winter. In the weeks leading up to the fairs, civic business was postponed, and householders made some useful cash letting rooms to visitors from all over the country.

The London fashion trade saw the Bristol fairs as a great showcase, and wholesalers of every kind of goods turned up from around the world to see what Britain had to sell. Poet Laureate Robert Southey, who was born in Bristol, went to one fair as a child where a shaved monkey was exhibited as a genuine

Fun of the fair. Until its suppression because of rowdy behaviour St James Fair was one of the great events of the year, not just for locals, but for people from all over the South-West.

fairy, and an equally hairless bear was dressed in checked coat and trousers, sat in a chair and labelled as an Ethiopian savage. The Bristol Great Fairs were abolished in 1838 when the thieving and bawdry became too much, even for cash-hungry Bristolians. As Latimer puts it primly: 'The decree put an end to saturnalia of which but a faint conception can be formed in our times.'

Bristol may have had two of the biggest but there were once fairs everywhere; Somerset alone had 94, including Shepton Mallet, where wives were once sold, but also where butchers from Bristol and Bath bought up to 400 fatted calves a day. Bath once had four fairs (one for the King, one for the bishop, one for the priory and one for the townsfolk) while the bishop also got the profits from Axbridge's lucrative St Barnabus' Fair. There were other famous events at Glastonbury, Wrington, Taunton, Bridgwater and most other places where people traditionally gathered to buy and sell.

Bristol remained a fair city, even after the decline of the two Great Fairs. Travelling showmen wintered here for years – Billy Butlin began his showbiz career with a Bristol fair – but few of the traditional fairs survive today.

Priddy still has its sheep fair, Chipping Sodbury its Mop, where servants were once hired, and Frome its cheese fair. Big events like the Royal Bath and West Show or the North Somerset Show are the real descendants of the Bristol Great Fairs, although the roguery, deception and outright sex are missing.

From grain storage to muddy waters

The Granary has played host to some of the biggest names in entertainment. It's also been deserted. And attempts to open a trendy restaurant on the ground floor seemed doomed to failure.

Venetian splendour. You could convince yourself that you were in Italy, but you'd be wrong! Welsh Back's magnificent Granary building, now converted into luxury flats, was built in the ornate Bristol Byzantine style although it was only ever planned as a warehouse.

Rock'n roll. Once the venue for many top rock acts, the Granary was also home to folk and jazz clubs.

Brickwork. The Granary of 1871 still has its original multi-coloured Cattybrook brickwork on show.

The ghost said to haunt the Granary has seen it all – jazz giants, the legends of rock, a dash of folk, Bristol's first wine bar, offices and, of course, the grain that gave the spectacular building its name.

It's a remarkably striking building and certainly the finest on the city waterfront. Unfortunately, no one has so far been able to find a way to use it all properly and still make money.

Upstairs, it has low ceilings and little natural light which limits commercial interest, but which has now been taken over by waterside apartments. But various schemes to make the ground floor and basement available for public use have sadly foundered.

The first ultra-trendy Belgo mussels and waffles restaurant outside London opened there and was very popular. But that closed to be replaced by a more restrained and formal restaurant, which also found competition with the many established local eateries too tough to challenge.

The ghost alleged to wander the lonely seven storeys is that of a Victorian workman. He is supposed to have been involved in an argument with a workmate over a woman and in the ensuing struggle fell down a lift shaft.

The Granary was built in 1871 as just that, a place for the storing and drying of grain. All those ornate openings helped circulate air around the grain to stop it going mouldy. Those were the days when the design of a building was as important as its functional ability. So the architect used local red, yellow and black Cattybrook brick and a lot of inspiration from Venice to create a wonderful building that has, thankfully, been tastefully restored. If you've ever heard the phrase Bristol Byzantine and wondered what it was, look at the Granary. It's the best example in the city of this school of architecture, even though, confusingly, it's really Venetian.

But if you were around in the 1960s, none of this mattered. In those days, the Granary was the place to see and be seen. Jazzman Acker Bilk first gave it a new lease of life when he opened his famous jazz club on the first two floors. International jazz and blues stars played there; I recall one stunning set by Chicago bluesman Muddy Waters who found the atmosphere far better than at his previous Bristol gig at the Colston Hall.

It cost £3 a year to join (£5 for couples) and the club offered a stage, dance floor and one of the longest bars in town. The Avon Cities Jazz Band was resident and Acker and his famous mates played regularly. But jazz couldn't really sustain such a huge place, especially with the rival Old Duke nearby, so there were rock nights too. Status Quo appeared there. So did Thin Lizzy, Yes, Curved Air, Elkie Brooks and Robert Plant among many others. There was also the New Grain Folk Club on Sundays with a massive membership fee of 50p a year.

Al Read, then resident DJ, said in 1975: 'Our genuine enthusiasm for quality live music has, over the years, made the Granary into the most successful music club in the West Country'.

Eventually, inevitably, the expense of running the old building led to jazz gradually dying out and rock taking over. Then that, too, was finally silenced. Since then there have been numerous plans for the Granary. Offices have been built upstairs, but the ground floors (reserved for public use) have been lined up for a theme pub, wine bar, night clubs, restaurants and a casino.

Most foundered because not enough people lived nearby, but that has now changed with students taking over former office blocks, and warehouses across the river being converted into flats. All of a sudden, the Granary is at the heart of one of the liveliest parts of Bristol, with new bars and restaurants complementing existing favourites like the River Station, Severn Shed and Renato's. Sadly, it has yet to find the right recipe for its own lower floors.

Cellars. Wooden sledges pulled by horses had been used in Bristol's narrow streets for generations. Despite the inconvenience, wheeled traffic was banned on the grounds that it would damage the vaults beneath the pavements.

Bristol, city of mud and smells

Bristol is a filthy city, plagued by endless traffic, and lacking in taste or any real commitment to the arts. The streets are badly lit, the council arrogant and uncaring, the people dull and think of nothing but making money.

Is this the Bristol you know and love? Surely not. These were, in fact, the results of a survey of the city taken in autumn 1798.

Yes, 205 years ago, they were already complaining about the traffic, and that was long before there were even any bus or cycle lanes. In those days, the problem wasn't delivery vans and lorries: it was delivery sledges. Wheeled transport was banned above the many cellars, which undermined the centre of the city around the harbour for fear of them caving in. Contemporary documents give a distinct impression that there was more concern for the wine stored beneath than anyone getting hurt.

Nevertheless, a writer to *The Monthly Magazine* condemned the barbarous custom of using sledges in the public streets for the carriage of goods which 'are continually endangering the limbs of both men and cattle'.

Cattle? Oh yes. Herds of cows and pigs were still driven through the narrow city streets on their way from farms and ships to the slaughterhouse. They, in turn, left considerable piles of evidence of their passing to add to the chaos. 'The city and its environs are much infested by such irregularities' thundered Felix Farley's *Journal*, which ran regular campaigns against the dirty city. 'Pigs, goats and other animals are suffered to wander about the streets with impunity'.

Animal droppings were one problem; so were the huge heaps of mud allowed to build up on the roads. This was the era of long dresses and elegant buckled shoes, and even the shortest walk in a city with virtually no pavements was far removed from the average television costume drama, where skirts remain clean and sweet smelling. If the streets were bad, what was even worse is that residents couldn't actually see what they were stepping in. There were streetlights of a sort, which produced 'a visible obscurity', according to one report, but they were pitifully inadequate and usually out by 8 p.m.

The corporation, which was then self-elected and answerable only to itself, was in those days far more interested in eating, drinking and partying than actually administering the city. When the mayor and aldermen held manor courts at Portishead, a goodly supply of claret and sack (sherry) was provided. Even so, the city worthies needed an initial refresher at the Failand Inn en route, another on the way back and a final top-up at Rownham. There was a banquet after every meeting and a feast every quarter. A barrel or two of wine was cracked every time an important document was signed, war declared or a civic visit arranged. It was a pretty good job being a councillor and the gang wanted to keep it so. Ludicrously, it was this which kept Bristol dark, dirty and dangerous.

Ratepayers (wealthy property owners then) were happy to pay extra to have the city cleaned up and policed, but only if the cash was administered by elected representatives. The corporation, worried about its ancient privileges, refused, and demanded control of the money. It was so hated and distrusted that no one would pay, so the city remained a festering sore.

In these conditions there didn't seem much reason for going out, which is possibly why Bristol was regarded as the dullest, most boring city in England. Felix Farley's *Journal* of 200 years ago recounted: 'The deficiency of public amusements in this populous and opulent city is not only a constant source of complaint to persons visiting it, but is also the subject of frequent regret to a great number of respectable inhabitants'.

A letter writer to *The Monthly Magazine* added: 'Perhaps there is no place in England where public and social amusements as so little attended to as here'. He blamed it on the citizens' love of moneymaking and the large number of non-conformist chapel-goers in the city.

The corporation lived up to its reputation in the face of such criticism – it launched a campaign against billiards, one of the few public amusements available. The mayor personally smashed up two billiard tables in the Exchange and threatened to do the same to every other in the city!

Queen uses phone – sensation!

It's more than 40 years since the Queen launched a telephone revolution from Bristol with a phone call to Edinburgh.

But what did she say?

For such a technological landmark, it has to be said that the conversation didn't live up to the standards of a Churchillian blood-stirrer speech or even an Oscar Wilde *bon mot*.

The Queen was in Bristol to launch the first Subscriber Trunk Dialling (STD) link. That may not seem terribly exciting these days, but making phone calls before STD was a laborious business, often involving several Hello Girls. STD was a fully automatic system, meaning telephone operators were no longer needed at exchanges – and it all began here.

If you are interested, the *Evening Post* recorded that the very first phone number dialled by the Queen was 031 CAL 3636. (Notice the alphabetical code, which responds to 225 on a modern keypad. In those days, you could tell where someone lived by the code, the best known of which

was Scotland Yard: WHI 1212. Alphabetical codes were later replaced by figures which usually corresponded to the letters on the dial to save confusion). It took just seconds before the phone was ringing in Edinburgh and was answered by the Lord Provost.

The conversation, again recorded for posterity by the *Evening Post*, continued like this:

The Queen: 'This is the Queen speaking from Bristol. Good afternoon, my Lord Provost.

Lord Provost: 'Good afternoon, Your Majesty. May I with humble duty offer you the loyal greetings of the citizens of Edinburgh'.

The Queen: 'Thank you, and would you, Lord Provost, please convey my greetings to them. I am always interested in any development which brings my people closer together'.

She added: 'In a few moments, Bristol subscribers will be able to make trunk calls by merely dialling the right number up to a distance of some 300 miles.

'In time the whole United Kingdom will enjoy the advantages of this new service which the Post Office has introduced'.

Hardly spontaneous but this, believe it or not, was the first time the Queen had ever personally dialled a call and the occasion was the first time a monarch had been photographed using a phone. Civilisation tottered.

That first STD call lasted two minutes five seconds, which would have cost 1s 5d – roughly 7p and higher than today. Under the old-fashioned Hello Girl system, it would have cost 3s 9d – around 18p. The reason for the fall in cost overnight was that, under the old system, phone calls had a three-minute minimum charge. STD allowed telephone users to be charged in 2d units instead, which meant calls lasting under three minutes became immediately cheaper.

Phone a friend. A young-looking Queen Elizabeth inaugurates the STD (Subscriber Trunk Dialing) system from Bristol's telephone exchange in 1958. The call went straight through to Edinburgh.

After her friendly chat with the Lord Provost, the Queen threw a switch which connected the 18,000 subscribers on Bristol Central exchange to the new system. Even then, they could only reach around half the rest of the country on STD. The following year, new coin boxes were introduced in kiosks, opening up the limited STD system to public phone users.

If you wonder why Bristol was chosen for the first STD exchange, it was probably because the city has always been a communications pioneer. The first mail coach service ran from Bristol to London and the city had one of the very first telephone exchanges, set up as long ago as 1879. It also had the first central battery exchange, the forerunner of all large manual exchanges.

Agapemone

Please stand for My Lord the Agapemone, the Keeper of the Seven Stars and the Seven Golden Candlesticks, and his Abode of Love in Somerset.

The Agapemonites were the idea of the Revd Henry James Prince who, on New Year's Day 1846, in Weymouth, Dorset, declared himself to be the Messiah. He was reported to the Home Secretary for impersonating the Almighty and for receiving his worshippers 'naked in body but veiled'. Three of them went mad and the people of Weymouth attacked him and his followers with stones.

Before that, he was the curate at Charlynch, Somerset, where he caused havoc by dividing his congregation into the saved and the damned. The result, as he happily boasted in his parish newsletter, was that 'husbands threatened to murder their wives; wives threatened to forsake their husbands'.

He then managed to gain a considerable fortune by persuading five rich sisters to marry his followers. When their family fought back and prosecuted him for obtaining cash by false pretences, he actually claimed in court to be descended from Adam, Noah and Jesus. With the cash he built a rather splendid mansion, which he called the Agapemone (Abode of Love) in the little village of Spaxton, Somerset, and persuaded many rich people to sever all connections with their families and withdraw from the world to the Agapemone to await the day of Judgment.

Local tradesmen used to address their bills to 'My Lord the Agapemone and Prince'. He travelled in a carriage attended by outriders, protected by bloodhounds and preceded by a man in purple livery calling out 'Blessed is he who cometh in the name of the Lord'

It gets better. He turned up at the Great Exhibition of 1851 in a coach bought from Dowager Queen Adelaide, wearing scarlet robes trimmed with white ermine and a crown. His second in command was known as Keeper of the Seven Stars and the Seven Golden Candlesticks.

The walls around the Agapemone were very high to keep strangers out and (it was often alleged) to stop the inmates escaping. Only female followers lived in the house; men were relegated to estate cottages. Prince was addressed as 'Beloved' at all times and when one of his followers became pregnant, he blamed it on the devil.

He considered it his divine duty to have first crack at any virgins, which he did in front of his followers (with the girls in white robes and himself in scarlet) on a couch in front of the altar. One rumour was that Prince placed his ladies on a revolving stage, which was then spun. Whoever stopped opposite him was Mrs Prince for the week. Sadly however, the Beloved failed to keep his promises and actually died in 1899. He was buried in the garden, standing upright.

Bristol boundaries

The city council called it expansion. Villagers regarded it as land-grabbing. But Bristol expanded remorselessly in the early years of the last century.

Districts around Bristol are constantly prepared for a fight over what the city sees as natural growth, but which call invasion.

These days, Bristol's territorial ambitions have been put on the backburner, despite obvious anomalies under which other councils make decisions which can have huge effects on the city, like the development of Cribbs Causeway and Abbey Wood.

Few people, especially newcomers, realise how many suburbs of Bristol were independent villages until the 1930s and even later. By the end of the nineteenth century,

Smiling Somerset. Few people can now recall the days when villages like Brislington were tranquil havens outside the city boundaries.

Cotham, Clifton, Redland, Brislington and the places to the east of Lawfords Gate were still outside the city. Hundreds of better-off Bristolians moved out of the dirty, smelly centre and into what were then attractive villages or smart new estates.

The city council was not pleased – it saw the refugees as enjoying all the benefits of Bristol while paying nothing towards them. It's an argument which has rumbled on ever since.

In 1891, Bristol bid for Horfield, Stapleton, St George, Hanham, Shire-hampton and parts of Mangotsfield, Oldham, Bedminster, Long Ashton, Henbury and Westbury-on-Trym. Locals objected fiercely, as did Gloucestershire and Somerset county councils, and Bristol backed off. Three years later it tried again, this time with a Parliamentary Bill, aimed at most of the same area plus Dunball Island, a tiny part of Somerset isolated by a change in the course

of the Avon. Once again there was a fight, which uncannily foreshadows the current objections to Bristol spreading. Bristol got all the poor areas in its land claim, but not wealthy Westbury and Henbury. Sneyd Park, Stoke Bishop and north Horfield also kept their freedom and lower rates.

It didn't last. Bristol spread remorselessly (but logically), and all the once independent parishes were swept up, one by one. Brislington (once described as one of the prettiest villages in north Somerset) lasted until 1933; Henbury until 1935, and Bishopsworth until 1956.

A few years ago, during the last re-organisation of local government, Bristol regained its own independence as a city and county and suggested it should take over the urban areas of Kingswood, Filton, Patchway and the vast new housing areas of Bradley Stoke. The bid failed, even though the boundaries between Bristol and Kingswood or Filton are little more than lines down streets dividing high rate council tax payers from low rate ones.

Perhaps if Bristol had won, it could have repeated a ceremony of 1900 to persuade new residents they were now part of the city. It was decided to hold a formal 'perambulation of the city boundaries', a trip which lasted a fortnight by foot, carriage and steamer. At various places, there were bumpings to mark the boundaries and no one was safe – even the Lord Mayor and a hapless baby were bounced up and down. On the final day, 250 people boarded the steamer *Britannia* to fix the water boundaries. They landed at Shirehampton and Portishead to mark the line between Bristol and Gloucestershire and Bristol and Somerset respectively, and on Steep Holm and Flat Holm islands to stake Bristol's claim.

Being in Bristol might have been more costly but there were benefits like street lighting, sewerage and police, which the suburbs lacked. And there was a fire brigade. In 1906 the Elm Tree Inn at Bishopsworth burned down. The city fire brigade refused to turn out because it was outside the boundary and city ratepayers were not affected.

World's first workhouse

St Peter's Hospital was a beautiful building that vanished in the Bristol Blitz. But it was also a sugar refinery, a mint and the world's first workhouse.

Confirmation that Bristol sailors really did discover America caused little stir among Bristolians, who always regarded Columbus as a bit of a tourist anyway. But Bristol also has another claim to fame which isn't boasted about quite so often. In 1698, the city set up the world's first workhouse.

Later generations knew it better as St Peter's Hospital, a remarkably beautiful half-timbered building which was destroyed by German bombs in 1941. Yet in the 500 years of its history, the building housed alchemists, a mint, some of Bristol's most famous merchant princes and sugar.

The first recorded reference to it was in 1402, when it was sold to Thomas Norton, bailiff, sheriff, mayor and MP for Bristol around the beginning of the fifteenth century. A later Thomas Norton was an alchemist, and spent his life searching for immortality and the way to make gold. He died in poverty, so presumably was unsuccessful on both counts.

In 1607 the house was brought by Robert Aldworth, a sugar refiner, who pulled down two thirds of it and built what older Bristolians still remember as St Peter's. Aldworth refined sugar in the eastern wing and the place became known as the Sugar House until 1696, when the then owners (including Edward Colston) turned it into a mint for making silver coins.

Two years later, Britain's first Poor Law Authority bought it, and it remained a workhouse until 1930 when the Corporation took it over. When it opened, Dr Thomas Dover offered free medical care. But he got fed up with doctoring, went off to be a pirate and was in charge of the privateer *Duke* which rescued Alexander Selkirk – the man who may have inspired Robinson Crusoe.

In its heyday, the workhouse must have been a terrible place. It was bought as a home for 100 boys; but by the beginning of the nineteenth century there were between 300 and 600 people of both sexes living in appalling conditions.

In 1832, cholera swept the city and 71 of the overcrowded inmates of St Peter's died. No wonder: the girls' ward had 10 beds and 58 inmates; the boys' ward had 80 inmates in 16 beds.

Blitzed loss. The workhouse building, home to generations of poor families, was at the heart of medieval Bristol.

Gabled gem. St Peter's Hospital, an ancient wonderfully decorated building, was lost to the city during a Nazi wartime raid. In its time it had housed an alchemist, a sugar refinery and a mint, and Britain's first workhouse.

Workhouse. Another view of St Peter's Hospital showing its position right next to St Peter's church on what is now Castle Park.

Times did improve. A Bristol newspaper report from the early 1930s recorded: 'The Poor Law of today takes care of the poor much more tenderly than was thought necessary in 1696 and no person need starve.'

A few years later, the beautiful hospital was in ruins and 500 years of history was at an end.

Floating harbour fight

Bristol city planners nearly destroyed Bristol in the '60s with a series of disastrous plans to create another Birmingham. Then the residents decided enough was enough.

The seeds of the citizen's revolt that scuppered the mediocre Crest Nicholson plan for Bristol harbourside were planted in 1969. That was the year the city planners came up with a plan which was so breathtakingly awful it scarcely seems credible today. They wanted to fill in the Floating Harbour and Feeder canal.

This was a council that wanted a hotel in Avon Gorge, a roundabout on The Downs, and to rip up much of Clifton, Cotham, Montpelier, Easton, Totterdown and Bedminster for a monstrous outer-circuit road with tunnels, flyovers and giant roundabouts. It built Broadmead, Britain's worst big city shopping centre, and tore down hundreds of historic buildings that had survived the war. Even worse, decisions were taken in secret and Bristolians were told to accept what experts had decided was best for them.

But, in the late '60s, and to the councillors' horror, their normally docile subjects rebelled. The Gorge Hotel plan was thrown out, and the outer-circuit road plan held up (and finally killed) by the fiercest public inquiry ever seen in Bristol. The planners fought back by announcing without warning that the ancient city docks were to close and navigation rights cancelled. That might have been acceptable; the additional idea of filling in the Floating Harbour was not.

The news was announced rather casually in the council's Civic News of August 1969. The master plan was to fill in the stretch of water from the Cumberland Basin locks to the junction of St Augustine's Reach and the whole Feeder canal; to use the land for offices, workshops and warehouses, and to drive the outer-circuit road through the middle.

Another road down The Grove would then cut through the Shakespeare pub in Prince Street and cross the Reach and Canons Marsh to a big new roundabout at the bottom of Jacobs Wells Road. Once again, there was a citizens' rebellion. A series of public meetings were held with professionals of all disciplines offering their services to fight the plan. Amenity societies, from the Civic Society to the Inland Waterways Association, united to fight a scheme aimed to destroy what was once Britain's premier west-coast port.

The council fought back strongly, insisting the closure was essential if the old docks area was to be used for public enjoyment. There were dire warnings that this was the only way forward and that delay would be fatal – a theme echoed many times since then.

Bristol MP Arthur Palmer managed to get the Bristol Docks Bill amended in the Commons to prevent any reduction in water surface and to preserve navigation rights for small boats.

The council responded by appointing Sir Hugh Casson as consultant for the redevelopment. Unfortunately, Sir Hugh came out strongly against the whole idea of big new roads across the docks.

Opposition grew even more fiercely after the *Evening Post* organized another public meeting and campaigners united in the Bristol Docks Group. Support for the fight came from across the country as the battle became national news. But the most important breakthrough came with the astonishing public welcome for the return of the SS *Great Britain* in the face of council apathy; the outspoken support of Prince Philip for the restoration of its old dock, and a series of successful water festivals and powerboat races.

The Arnolfini led the way in showing how old dockside buildings could be reused and others soon followed. The council finally caved in, abandoned the bill and gave the public what it wanted – an open harbour with plenty of public access and interesting developments around it.

It was a long hard battle and one which forced the council to become more open and actually ask the public what it wanted instead of arrogantly imposing the ideas of a few upon the city. But the battle isn't completely won – public opinion lost the battle to have the river beneath the Centre opened up again and Bristol was given a bleak civic water feature instead. Public rebellion stopped the dismal Canons Marsh redevelopment, but an amended version is going ahead. As Sir Hugh Casson said after the docks battle: 'What has happened is the beginning of a customers' revolt – a refusal any longer to be totally the victim of experts, a growing insistence on having more say in the shape of our surroundings'.

Bristol gaols

Conditions in Bristol's prisons were once bad beyond belief, which is why felons preferred to be banged up in Lawford's Gate Gaol where they were treated humanely.

In 1812, James Neild, High Sheriff, Justice of the Peace and Treasurer of the Society for the Relief of Persons Imprisoned for Small Debts, published a book called *State of Prisons in England, Scotland and Wales*. These were the

Gaol. All that remains of the old Cumberland Road gaol, destroyed by the mob at the time of the Bristol riots, but in use until 1883.

days when you could end up in prison for years for the smallest debt, as recorded by Charles Dickens in Little Dorrit, and unless you had someone to provide decent food from outside, life could be bleak. Some of the conditions Neild discovered on his tours in prisons were almost beyond belief; in others, life was better than that enjoyed by the average family outside.

Neild visited three Bristol prisons – Newgate, Bridewell and Lawford's Gate (which was then in Gloucestershire). In Newgate and Lawford's Gate, he found a complete contrast between the brutality of one and the enlightened conditions of the other.

Newgate City and County Gaol

Gaoler William Humphries was paid £200, another £2 a year gown-money plus fees for debtors. The chaplain, the Revd Mr Day, got £35 for a sermon each Sunday and prayers on Wednesdays and Fridays. The number of prisoners on October 4, 1803, was 24 debtors, 26 felons and two deserters. Debtors were given no free food; felons were allowed a three-penny loaf of standard wheat bread.

'This Gaol, called Newgate, is build on a declivity, and stands in the middle of the City' reported Neild.

'It is very antique, and by much too small for the general number of its inhabitants. The lower rooms are dark. For Debtors there are about 15 large and airy rooms; two of which are termed free wards for poor Debtors, who find their own beds.

'These rooms pay two shillings and six pence per week each; and two Prisoners sleep in a bed. Here is not a proper separation of Men and Women'.

The only exercise area – known as the Tennis Court – was just 13 yards by six and also used for drying linen. There was a pump with drinking water and a convenient bath which, James Neild noted, was 'seldom used'.

Male felons had two small day rooms and sleeping rooms with little air or light. But the worst horror of all was the Pit.

'The Pit to which you descend by eight steps, is 17 feet in diameter, and 8 feet 6 inches high. It has barrack bedsteads, with beds of straw in canvass; and some benevolent Gentlemen of the City occasionally send a few rugs.

'This dreary place is close and offensive; with only a very small window, whose light is merely sufficient to make darkness visible. In the year 1801, it was chiefly appropriated to convicts under sentence of transportation. Seventeen prisoners are said to have slept here every night!

'The Turnkey himself told me that in a morning, when he unlocked the door, he was so affected by the putrid steam issuing from the dungeon, that it was enough to strike him down. When Turnkeys are thus affected by only opening the doors, what must the pitiable wretches suffer, confined, through the whole night, in such fetid hotbeds of disease'.

The prison was full of narrow passages, which were kept as clean as possible and scraped and whitewashed once a year. Prisoners depended on charity, such as the £4 9s left by Mr Freeman, for bread and beef on Christmas Eve. Local churchwardens also paid £4 2s towards prisoners' upkeep.

James Neild was upset by the small numbers attending church services and the behaviour in chapel.

'So little regard, indeed, was paid to the Chapel, as a place of worship, that I have repeatedly seen the prisoners drinking,

Lawfords Gate. This old prison was at the end of Old Market and, after over 100 years in use, was finally demolished in 1907.

The Spike. Another view of the Cumberland Road prison. It opened its gates in 1820.

Inside. An insiders view of Lawfords Gate prison, with the heavy swivel gate open.

smoking and chewing tobacco in the gallery. He added: 'Several years since, an Act was passed for the building of a new Gaol. That it has not been carried into execution by this rich commercial City, is much to be regretted; for, really the present Gaol is disgraceful.'

Neild also showed unusual concern for hapless debtors, thrown into the same prison as murderers and thieves – legal suffering, as he called it. 'How often do we overlook that most lamentable groupe, which it so dreadfully oppresses! – I mean the victims of mere misfortune, the feeble and unresistless sacrifices to false and groundless accusation!'

Lawford's Gate: The County Bridewell

The keeper here was Joseph Hallam, who was paid £50 a year with no fees. The chaplain, the Revd Mr Eden, got £20 as year for sermons and prayers and the prison had a salaried surgeon who received £15 15s. On December 17, 1801, there were nine prisoners, each given a loaf of one good household bread every day.

'This Prison was finished in 1791. The boundary wall encloses about an acre of ground, and affords the Keeper a convenient garden for the growth of vegetables.

'On the right of the Gate is a room, where the Magistrates hold their Petty Session. The approach to the Prison is through a small garden, separated from the courtyards by close wooden palisades.

'Here are four airy courts, of 28 yards by 15, with a pump and a sewer in each; and three day-rooms. 13 feet by 11 feet 6, with fire-places, stone seats and shelves. The Women's court has a grass-plat, to bleach and dry the linen'.

Sleeping quarters were equally impressive – nine cells for women and 10 for men on each floor, each measuring 7 feet 4 inches by 6 feet 1, and 10 feet high, 'with an arched roof, to prevent danger and confusion in case of fire'. Each was fitted up with a cast-iron bedstead, straw-mat, hair-mattress, a blanket, sheet, and double rug and had light and ventilation. Two cells for vagrants were provided with straw, which was regularly replaced.

'On this upper-story are also two infirmary rooms, with fire-places and water-closets; and three small rooms used as foul-wards, from which iron-gratings communicate with the Chapel, to accommodate the sick Prisoners for hearing Divine service.

'Here is likewise a Dispensary for the Surgeon; and all these latter apartments have glazed windows'.

All prisoners were made to attend church services but debtors and felons were kept separate. They were also provided with warm and cold baths, an oven to 'purify the prisoners' clothes', free prison uniforms, and four stoves which heated the whole building in winter.

If there was work available, prisoners got a cut of their earnings to buy extra food. Any money left over was saved for them and paid when they were discharged, but prisoners who refused to work were put into solitary confinement. Medical care was probably better than most ordinary Bristol folk received, with the surgeon seeing each prisoner once a week and always available when requested. He also had the power to suspend punishment or vary diets and careful record was kept of his observations for the Visiting Justices. There were even books, admittedly of 'moral and religious instruction', and 'proper cisterns, with soap and towels, are supplied to each courtyard, near the pump, for the daily use of the Prisoners. Weights and measures also are kept for their use; and they have clean linen once a week'.

World beaters. The superb Bristol 400 series of cars are all craftsman built at the company's Filton works.

Bristol Cars

It's a little-known story but Bristol Cars saved BMW of Germany from ruin in the years after the Second World War.

Bristol Cars and BMW are rivals today in the dignified but ferocious market for luxury, up-market cars. But they were once partners and, according to one of BMW's most famous designers, could have produced a world-beater together.

BMW – it stands for the German equivalent of Bavarian Motor Works – started making aircraft engines and motorcycles – and British Austin Sevens under licence! But its own cars, especially the sports models, were classics.

The Second World War left BMW in ruins and its factories split by the division of Germany into East and West. It might have folded – except for Bristol Cars.

BMWs had been imported before the war, by the Aldington brothers company, AFN, and sold as Frazer Nash BMWs. The Aldingtons renewed links with Munich when the war ended, but it was obvious BMW would be unable to supply cars for some time. But Bristol Aeroplane Company was thinking about turning to car building to replace the aircraft orders it would lose with the end of the war. One of the Aldingtons had a BMW Mille Miglia sports car – and Bristol fell for it. BAC bought a majority stake in AFN and engineers visited BMW in Munich, officially to inspect high-altitude test facilities. But they quietly brought back technical details of the BMW 326, 327 and 328 models, plus two engines.

It was the start of a remarkable Euro-partnership, years before the Common Market. The car plans became an official war reparation and BMW engineering director Fritz Fiedler was invited to Bristol.

The first joint model, unveiled in Geneva in 1947, was the Bristol 400, which bore a remarkable resemblance to the BMW 327, right down to the grille and badge. The 400 reached 70mph in a less-than-blistering 30 seconds, and cost £2,723. The very first one off the line was later bought by Tony Crook, the former racing ace who took over the company in 1973. Almost every component was made at the Filton works – and made to aircraft quality. The 400s, of which just 700 were made, were noted for their road holding and won a number of world class rally events.

Bristol soon gained its own strong identity, still with BMW engineering at its heart. Bodies were styled by top designers and the emphasis was always on quality.

Baron Alex von Falkenhausen, a leading light of the modern BMW, now regrets that the BMW-Bristol link wasn't developed.

'The Bristol company made the BMW engine with better materials and it was very successful – especially in Formula B racing, with Cooper. The best thing for AFN would have been for the Aldingtons to supply Bristol engines and for me to make the car. It would have been unbeatable.'

The 400s success in rallies led to Bristol opening a racing department. A coupe was developed in the Filton wind tunnel which did 142mph on the Brabazon runway. Better results followed, but by 1955, the engine had had its day and the racing department closed. Bristol cars became more luxurious and less sporty, and in 1963 turned to American Chrysler engines for its new 407.

Bristol engines had been used in a number of other sports cars, especially the Cooper Bristol in which Mike Hawthorn made his name. The last car with the Bristol-BMW engine was the 1956 AC Ace – a true classic.

The cars are almost entirely hand-made and Bristol Cars turns out no more than three or four a week. It also restores all older models. All are very strong, yet very light for their size, thanks to a solid chassis coupled with aluminium body. And the latest model, the Blenheim, manages 30mpg despite its enormous 5.9 litre Chrysler V8 engine. It costs £110,000 with a top speed of 150mph and acceleration of 60mph in just 6.9 seconds.

Former Tory Cabinet ministers William Waldegrave and John Patten were both big Bristol fans. Patten described the marque as 'the archetype of Bristol discretion' and added: 'This discreet reverence is followed even in the correct naming of parts. The hubcaps are called nave plates, the badges crowning them roundels, as though this was the great Sir Nikolaus Pevsner on the crocketed spires of Huntingdonshire.

'Indeed some of the best Bristols were wooden framed, though in car-makers' ash, not the oak of cathedral builders.

'With Bristols, discretion is the overriding virtue. Name plates are so small they can hardly be seen.'

William Waldegrave, former MP for Bristol West, owns a classic Bristol 402 convertible.

'It was always my ambition as a boy to own a Bristol and I managed to buy one for £600 in 1973,' he said.

'My 402 is my pride and joy. I would never sell it and I will get myself a 404 if I ever win the lottery.'

The Bristol Blenheim brochure keeps the same spirit, advertising the car as 'dignified express travel for four six foot persons and their luggage.'

By 1963, when the last Ace was made, BMW was back on the road again and has never looked back. But without the help from Bristol, in the dark days after the war, one of the world's best-known cars would be little more than a memory.

White slaves

The theory that slaves were once imprisoned in Redcliffe caves and cellars around old Bristol has long since been disproved. Or has it?

Everyone thinks of black Africans when they talk about slaves. And it would indeed have been pointlessly costly to bring them to Bristol instead of straight to the colonies. But what about the white slaves, the thousands sent abroad over the centuries for rebellion, minor crimes or just being in the wrong place at the wrong time?

Bristol was notorious in medieval times for kidnapping passing strangers and selling them to the Irish as slaves. After the Civil War, Bristol merchants were given 500 Royalist prisoners by Cromwell to work on the West Indian plantations, and he later passed on hundreds of Irish rebels as well.

But the whole trade was quite corrupt as Francis Rawlings of Keys Avenue, Horfield, found when researching Bristol's other slave trade. In the memoirs of seventeenth-century Bristol Recorder Roger North, Francis found details of how aldermen and magistrates used the system to make considerable fortunes. A poor devil up on some minor charge which could put him on the gallows, was advised by a 'friendly' court official to beg for transportation instead. The frightened malefactor usually agreed. 'The game thus bagged was appropriated by the magistrates in rotation,' Francis discovered. 'There was sometimes squabbling as to who had first claim to the wretches being shipped off as marketable merchandise.'

But with hundreds of people waiting to be sold into slavery, where were they kept? Perhaps, thinks Francis, that's the origin of the tale of slaves being stored in Redcliffe caves and pub cellars. Maybe that was where the 850 transported from Judge Jeffreys' Bloody Assizes were imprisoned – and Bristol's mayor came very close indeed to joining them.

By the seventeenth century, Bristol was again notorious for kidnapping young residents from the streets and spiriting them off to the colonies. In 1654, the council passed a resolution condemning the selling of children as barbarous and wicked, and threatened heavy fines against any ship carrying unwilling passengers. What the council didn't mention was that their own members were heavily involved – and in 1685 the Mayor of Bristol, Sir William Hayman, was himself up before the dreaded Judge Jeffreys for sending a boy overseas. Jeffreys called Hayman 'a kidnapping knave' and told him 'You are worse than the pickpocket who stands at the bar.' He was fined £1,000, a fortune in those days.

Francis has also found a letter demonstrating how widespread slavery was. It was written in 1657 from the West Indies by a resident who begged his sister to find an indentured servant for him because they could be sold for a big profit.

'It is obvious from all this that the Bristol trade in slaves was well established before the African trade which commenced about 1860 and lasted until about 1769,' Francis added. Bristol did indeed have a bad record for enslaving black Africans – but it had a far worse one for selling its fellow countrymen. Just ask the thousands of people all over the world descended from the wretches sold into slavery by their fellow citizens.

New Church

The New Church on Cranbrook Road, Redland, may be Bristol's smallest, but it's not the most apathetic by any means.

It's distinctly possible you've never heard of the New Church. Yet for exactly a century, this tiny place of worship has stood quietly in Cranbrook Road on the bank of the old Cran Brook.

The congregation these days is tiny – the New Church has a national membership of just 1,412 and Bristol is one of only 32 congregations. Services in Cranbrook Road attract an average of four to six people.

The New Church was started in 1783 by followers of philosopher and mystic Emmanuel Swedenborg who claimed to have talked with angels and visited Heaven, and who wrote some very long books.

The Bristol church – the New Jerusalem Temple – began in 1792, the year that the president of the national New Church Conference was a Bristol layman called Anthony Hunt. But the early years were plagued with dissension and heavy debt. In 1819, a new church was opened in Silver Street but a breakaway group was founded in the Horsefair. The church was destroyed in the Bristol Riots of 1831 and the New Church in Bristol was effectively moribund for many years. It was revived following the success of the church in Bath and lectures in the Princes Street Assembly Rooms in Bristol which attracted around a thousand people.

The Bristol society first met behind what is now the Colston Hall, then in rented premises in the Triangle, Clifton, and the Oddfellows Hall, Rupert Street. But although the congregation shrank by half, the New Church's first permanent home was opened in Terrell Street (now the site of Bristol Royal Infirmary) in 1878.

It was something of a poor relation in a city full of great religious buildings – 'a small plain iron building in an almost unknown and uninviting street in the midst of a great city filled with noble churches', as one minister put it rather glumly. A stone frontage was added later but it was still what another minister called disparagingly 'a tin church with a false façade'.

Still, there was a minor scandal in 1890 when the minister, the Revd C.H. Wilkins, was forced to resign for taking spiritual comfort to a Mrs Davis rather too often, for too long and at what were called 'unseemly hours'.

The church planned a new building in Terrell Street and built up close links with the new Church in Australia. But the infirmary needed the land to expand and the church was sold. The money was used to build a new church in Cranbrook Road, near the new suburb of Bishopston, and it opened on Christmas Day 1899.

The church flourished in the early years of the twentieth century and even the Sunday school had 75 pupils in 1917. But that year, the minister, the Revd G. Meek, was accused of taking a much bigger salary than he was due. His salary was suspended amid allegations of unpaid bills and broken promises and by the time the row was settled, the war and the drift of families out of Bristol had seriously affected church attendances. A new minister , the Revd William Bates, seems to have disapproved of women's activities, especially the flourishing Girl Guides which welcomed members from other churches. A letter from the time comments; 'It is unfortunate Mr Bates does not look with a more kindly eye upon the Girl Guide movement, otherwise with tact many of these girls might have been brought in'.

By 1939 the church was thriving, only to be hit by another war. Even the once wealthy Bath congregation was forced to sell its fine premises in Henry Street (now restored by Bath University) and meet in a converted telephone exchange.

The Bristol New Church now shares a minister with Bournemouth, but still houses a library dating back to 1790 and the magic lantern which once attracted big crowds.

As Neil Marchant comments in *Like a Great River Flowing – The Story of the Bristol Society of the New Church*:

Cranbrook Road: The New Church in Redland was founded by the followers of mystic Emmanuel Swedenborg.

'It is at time dispiriting to be so few but the church continues to be enthusiastic as it faces the centenary of worship in Cranbrook Road. It is not clear for how long the Bristol Society will survive, but we can be thankful for the rich heritage of the church and for its influence on the city of Bristol'.

Portishead Radio

Portishead Radio was the link for nearly a century between Britain and the world's shipping. But it closed with the introduction of new technology that made its short-wave transmissions redundant.

As the Great War ended the General Post Office (GPO) began to reopen short-range wireless stations which linked coastal ships with the shore. But there was still no way of sending or receiving messages from long-distance shipping. Then, in 1919, the GPO teamed up with the Marconi Wireless Telegraph Company to convert a redundant Imperial Wireless Chain receiving station at Devizes for long range use. Station GKT opened in 1920 with a range of 1,500 miles from its six kilowatt valve transmitter.

GKT was based in old army huts and could transmit telegrams to and from ships up to five days steaming from a British port for 11d a word. The service was so successful a second transmitter was built at Devizes and a new receiving site was opened at Burnham-on-Sea.

By 1926, short-wave wireless had transformed communications. The first maritime short-wave transmitter was again at Devizes and was highly successful. The following year, Devizes closed and a completely new transmitting station opened at Portishead. The service expanded dramatically and in the

'30s, messages from Portishead were relayed to South Africa and India by wireless operators on flying boats. This was the golden age of the great ocean liners which still used long-wave radios, and these messages, too, went through Portishead.

By 1936, Portishead Radio had three long wave and four short-wave transmitters, with its control and receiving centre at Burnham. It was handling well over three million words a year through a staff of 60 operators.

The war years brought great changes. Portishead sent messages to naval and merchant ships and received distress calls, enemy sighting reports, news of the North Africa landings and the sinking of the *Scharnhorst* and secret messages from the resistance in Europe.

By 1943, naval operators from HMS *Flowerdew* were called in to help the over-stretched civilian staff, and many Portishead staff were called up to man stations at home and abroad and train other staff. The station also set up a special division to communicate with aircraft patrolling the North Atlantic.

When the war ended, Portishead faced an overwhelming demand for long-range communication, and British and Commonwealth ships were able to use naval stations around the world to relay messages to Portishead.

Two new operating rooms were opened in 1948, with 32 operating positions, a broadcasting and land line room and a central control room with a 36ft x16ft steel map of the world. The centre kept track of many ships and aircraft using magnetic tags on the map and a special eye was kept on the liners when VIPs were on board.

Communication was still largely by hand-keyed Morse code until a telex service was introduced allowing customers to send and receive messages direct from the station. Some high volume users even had their own private circuits. Expansion continued into the '60s, with the first Telex Over Radio (TOR) and a Morse news service. By 1965, 86 operators were handling more than 11 million words a year and communicating with more than 1,000 ships each day.

In April 1970, the long-range radio-telephone service was transferred to Portishead and an additional control centre was opened at Somerton. And although naval business declined, there was a huge growth in calls for oil platforms, deep water fishermen, and long distance yacht racers. By 1974, the station was handling 20 million words a year and employed 154 operators.

The computer era and satellite communication brought even greater changes. A new building, including a computer-based message handling system, was opened at Burnham, while the growth of satellite traffic led to ground-based services having spare capacity for the first time since wireless telegraphy began.

Portishead transmitting station closed in the late '70s and in 1983, Portishead Radio moved to a new control centre at Burnham, although it still operated under the old name.

New technology speeded up messages, and direct ship-to-shore dialling was introduced, together with message storage and automated delivery. Sailors could also phone home via Portishead with calls billed to their UK phone number. In 1985, a new phone patch service was introduced for aircraft which also offered world-wide flight information.

Ships could access Portishead Radio's data bank for North Atlantic weather bulletins, news, sport, key financial information – even details of port congestion, berth availability and fuel prices. And the Gateway service offered a vital link between Britain and aid and charity workers and construction companies in remote parts of Africa.

But satellite communication made Portishead's venerable Morse code transmitters obsolete and by 1997, the station was receiving just 100 calls a day. The turn of the century saw

Morse finally phased out and replaced by a global distress and safety system. It was only a matter of time before Portishead Radio went the same way.

There are few signs of the old transmitting station now. The four 298ft tall masts and the eight 133 ft ones disappeared from the hill above Portishead in 1972 after 52 years as a landmark for Bristol Channel ships. Portishead Radio, which made the little town famous around the world, has fallen silent for the last time.

Armoury Square

The French once planned to burn Bristol and create havoc – but the wind blew them to Wales instead. But the episode gave rise to one of east Bristol's best-known streets.

Armoury Square in Easton is a quiet backwater off Stapleton Road – and a memorial to the last invasion of England. At least it would have been the last invasion of England if the wind hadn't been blowing in the wrong direction, which took the invasion fleet to Fishguard instead.

It happened during the war between Britain and the French after the French Revolution, which the English government feared would lead to similar uprisings in this country. It didn't happen, but war was declared anyway and around 1,200 French soldiers were gathered in Brittany with the aim of burning the port of Bristol – a project 'of the utmost importance'.

The idea was that the French would sail up the Avon after dark, set fire to the part of Bristol to windward, and let the wind do the rest. 'If the enterprise be conducted with dexterity', said the troop orders 'it cannot fail to produce the total ruin of the town, the port, the docks and the vessels and to strike terror and amazement into the very heart of the capital of England'.

But, as usual, God was on the side of the English and contrary winds blew the French over to Wales where they landed at Fishguard and were mopped up by local militia men.

But when Bristol discovered to its horror that it had been the real target, nearly 1,000 men rushed to join the new Bristol Volunteers and signal posts were erected on Brean Down, the Holm islands and Lavernock Point near Cardiff. A gun battery was built on Portishead Point and another at Avonmouth and gun-ships stationed in the Avon – just in time for peace to be declared.

But a year later, the war resumed and Bristol was supplied with extra guns for the Volunteers.

Fear of invasion was again growing and the government agreed to build a depot to store 20,000 guns on land just outside the city by what is now Stapleton Road. The depot contained a big armoury, two brick magazines for ammunition, storage, a workshop and guard house complete with cells for disobedient soldiers. There were houses for the officer of the Bristol garrison, the armourer and storekeeper, and a barracks for 24 soldiers, and the whole place was surrounded by a seven ft wide ditch. It must have been the cosiest posting in Britain with only the vegetable garden to tend, the notorious night life of Lawford's Gate five minutes away – and no sign of the enemy.

And that was it. The war ended in 1815 and two years later the soldiers left their peaceful life to continue their military careers. The armoury was then rented out for various purposes until 1831 when the Guardians of the Poor bought it for a new asylum for poor lunatics. It had a brief resurgence as a military base during the Bristol Riots when troops from Cardiff were based there, and the asylum then moved to Stapleton.

The whole armoury complex was finally sold for housing in what was first named Armoury Place in 1849 and finally Armoury Square in 1852. Some of the armour houses do still survive as nos 12,19, 39 and 46, and it was in no. 46 that Mr Packer began his famous chocolate company which is now in Greenbank. Nothing remains of the old armoury building but its memory is kept alive in the local pub, the Armoury Tavern.

A full and detailed history of the armoury and the square, with illustrations, appears in *Bristol's Vanished Georgian Armoury* and *The Development of Armoury Square* by John Bartlett and John Penny of Fishponds Local History Society.

Easton promise. Armoury Square, just off Stapleton Road, was built on the site of an old depot, hastily constructed to back up the local militia should a planned French invasion ever come to fruition.

Gone for ever. The demolition gangs of the 1960s gradually gave way to '70s conservation, and 20 homes in Armoury Square were saved.

Chocolate. The house in Easton's Armoury Square where Mr Packer started manufacturing his chocolates using just heat from a kitchen fire, old saucepans and paraffin lamps.